D1493578

THE CLOUD OF UNKNOWING
AND
THE LETTER OF PRIVATE DIRECTION

THE CLOUD OF
UNKNOWING
AND
THE LETTER OF
PRIVATE DIRECTION

Newly edited, with an Introduction by

ROBERT WAY

Published by

SOURCE BOOKS	‖	ANTHONY CLARKE
Trabuco Canyon		Wheathampstead
California USA		Hertfordshire England

The Cloud of Unknowing and *The Letter of Private Direction*
first published in this edition 1986 by
ANTHONY CLARKE PUBLISHERS, Wheathampstead,
Hertfordshire, England

Published in the United States of America by SOURCE
BOOKS, Trabuco Canyon, California.

ISBN 0 85650 075 5
ISBN 0 940147 017 (USA Edition)

First edition 1986
Reprinted 1994

Printed by Professional Book Supplies Ltd. Abingdon Oxon. England

Contents

Introduction

In 1871 Canon H. Collins published a book called *The Divine Cloud* which was a modernisation of *The Cloud of Unknowing*. This rescued *The Cloud of Unknowing* from a period of complete neglect lasting almost 250 years, ever since Fr. Augustine Baker in 1629 wrote a commentary on the work for use of the nuns of Cambrai for whom he was spiritual director.

Canon Collins's work was unfortunately vitiated by his using a bad manuscript of a late recension of the work.

It was forty years later in 1912 that Evelyn Underhill published a modernisation of the work under its proper title *The Cloud of Unknowing*.

In 1924 Dom Justin McCann published another modernisation together with *The Letter of Private Direction* and Fr. Augustine Baker's commentary on *The Cloud* itself.

In 1944 the original text of *The Cloud of Unknowing* together with *The Letter of Private Direction* was edited by Phyllis Hodgson for the Early English Texts Society. This text was based on that of the British Museum ms. Harl 674, a manuscript of the early fifteenth century together with the full collation of six other manuscripts. Phyllis Hodgson published a new edition of the text in the *Analecta Carthusiana*, Exeter 1982 but without the full critical apparatus. In the last sixty years an immense number of articles and books have been written on every aspect of *The Cloud of Unknowing* many are scholarly works, most notably William Johnston's *The Mysticism of the Cloud of Unknowing*,[1] but some of the others merit the admonition, in the words of our author; *"See here are many words but little substance"*.

The Cloud of Unknowing was written probably in the last

---

[1] published 1978/87 by Anthony Clarke

quarter of the fourteenth century in the East Midland dialect. The author remained, and still remains, anonymous, probably out of humility; considering the work to be the important thing, the author of no importance. The reason for his anonymity was certainly not, as Ira Progoff suggests, fear of being accused of heresy, for the author keeps emphasising the necessity of obeying all the ordinances of the church and indeed he attacks those who follow their own speculation rather than the common rules of the church. His anonymity was respected by his contemporaries and immediate successors, so leaving us with a impenetrable mystery. Only one serious suggestion regarding the authorship has been put forward, namely Walter Hilton who wrote *The Scale of Perfection*. This was the opinion of James Grenehalgh, a fifteenth century monastic scholar of Sheen Charterhouse, and there are indeed a number of similarities in the figures of speech of the two authors. But this is only to be expected of two people who shared a common theological and cultural background. If two different people start from the same point and go in the same direction it is likely that their account of the journey will have many similar descriptions. Further, Phyllis Hodgson shows (*Modern Language Review; October 1955*) that the figures of speech are used in completely different contexts and Father J. P. D. Clarke (*Downside Review vol. 95, 1977*) states that at decisive points the paths of the two authors divide and they use similar language in the interests of different theologies. It would be strange, too, if Hilton issued some of his works in his own name and others anonymously. what is more Hilton, at the end of his Angels' Song, attacks some aspects of *The Cloud's* teaching and it is hardly likely that he would attack his own work. Hilton and our author both came from the East Midlands and were probably contemporaries: it is likely that they read each others' books and they may even have known each other.

INTRODUCTION

Lacking all outside information we are left to glean what little we can from the work itself.

It seems clear that our author was a hermit: for his criticism of those who say that it is not lawful for men to set themselves to serve God in the contemplative life without first making provision for their bodily needs, and his statement that God provides those who rely on Him either with an abundance of necessities or strength of body and patience to do without them, are too clear and sincere not to spring from personal experience.

Further he equates himself with his pupil who is about to become a hermit.

There are indications that the author was a country gentleman before he received his call from God. It would only occur to a man who had had experience with hounds to use the simile of the greedy greyhound snatching its food and the metaphor of the leash. Also the custom of breaking the glass after a toast, expecially a royal toast, would only be met with in rich houses. There are, too, country metaphors from shooting. I see him as a scholarly country landowner who, on receiving his call from God, divesting himself of his worldly possessions, threw himself on the mercy of God and found He did not fail him. The blessing at the end of *The Cloud of Unknowing* does not prove that he was a priest but the fact that he was acting as a spiritual director makes it likely that he was. Clearly he was fond of children as we see from his similes of a father playing with his child and rescuing him from wild beasts and, more especially, in his account of the pleasing character of those who have the urge to follow the work of the *Letter*; where he says "what you wish for is the pleasure of playing with a child": a statement so clear and pleasing and yet many scholars will not accept it as it is and invent all sorts of amendments and explanations for it. One may well believe that the quiet of the author's hermitage was often broken by the sound of the voices of local children. The author gives us the impression of being an old man and he is much inclined to wander from his subject, as he himself acknowledges. Time and again we read "*but back to our subject*". Richard Methley a Carthusian who translated *The Cloud* into Latin in 1491 thought the author was a Carthusian. There has been much speculation on that point but certainly it would appear that up to the Reformation it was mainly in Carthusian houses that *The Cloud* was studied and copied.

Besides *The Cloud of Unknowing* and *The Letter of Private Direction* there are several other works almost certainly by the author. They are *Denis's Hid Divinity* a translation of *Dionysius Mystical Theology*, translated not from the original Greek, but from the Latin translation of Johannes Sarracenus with the help, as he himself says, of the commentary of Thomas Gallus abbot of St. Andrews Vercelli: *An Epistle of Prayer* and *Epistle of Discretion*, *A Treatise of Discerning of Spirits* based on a compilation of two of St. Bernard's sermons, and *A Treatise on the study of wisdom that men call "Benjamin"*, a précis of Richard St. Victor's *"Benjamin Minor"*. All but *The Discerning of Spirits* are claimed by the author in the seventh chapter of *The Letter of Private Direction*. The author follows the *via negativa* based on the works attributed to Dionysius the Aeropagite (mentioned in the *Acts of the Apostles* chapter 17) but now generally believed to have been written by an anonymous 5th century Syrian monk, who used Dionysius's name to give it authority. The work first appears in history when an appeal to its authority was made at the Council of Constantinople in 533. It first became known in Western Europe when a copy was sent by the Byzantine Emperor to King Louis of France in 827, and about 860 it was translated into Latin by the Irish scholar, John Scotus Erigena. The philosophy of the work is based on a Christianised Neoplatonism. God is too high and spiritual to be conceived by human minds. He is surrounded by darkness which is in fact an excess of divine light, as Dionysius says in his letter to Dorotheus the Deacon: "The divine darkness is the inaccessible light in which God dwells, and since He is invisible by reason of the overwhelming brightness and inaccessible through the supernatural excess of light, it follows that whoever deserves to know and see God, by the very fact that he neither sees nor knows Him, attains to that which is above sight and knowledge, and at the same time comes to know that God is beyond all perception and understanding".

God cannot be approached by knowledge but only in darkness by love and desire. The author calls this darkness the cloud of unknowing which always lies between man and his God except very occasionally when a ray of light pierces through and for an instant God reveals some of His secrets.

The idea of the cloud may come from Exodus (chapter 20) where Moses goes up to the dark cloud where God is or from Psalm 96 Verse 2 "Clouds and thick darkness are round about Him".

The image of the cloud hiding God from us is found in the eleventh sermon of Gregory of Nyssa (330–395). The author tells us that as well as the *The Cloud of Unknowing* which is above us, between us and our God, there is beneath us a cloud of forgetting into which we must trample down all thought and imagination which might interfere with our concentration on God. It is particularly important for us to consider the nature of "the work". Just to translate "the work" as contemplation is incorrect, for it is far more than that. The author says that it is the higher part of contemplation which, though it starts in this life, will continue on into eternity. The best way of translating it seems to be to keep the author's term "the work". The ultimate aim of the work is, as the author tells us early in *The Cloud*; "to knit himself to God in strict union of love and accordance of will". Man cannot come to this by his own endeavours but only through special grace, which God gives freely to whosoever He wishes without any merit on their part. All that we can do is to strike upon the cloud of unknowing with darts of love, loving God for Himself alone and not for His gifts (for God may be got and held by love, but by thought never). It is our part to put ourselves in a fit state to receive the special grace if it should please God to give it. This we must do by humility, cleansing ourselves of our sins by confession and exercising ourselves in the good deeds of active life and ordinary meditation.

This grace is nevertheless never missing if we truly desire it. For as *The Cloud* says (Chapter 34) "The capability for the work is inseparably united with the work itself, so that anyone who has a feeling for this work is able to do it and no-one else. Insomuch that without this work a soul is, as it were, dead and cannot covet or desire it by that amount that you will and desire it, to that amount that you will have it no more and no less". There are dire warnings for those who attempt the work without this special grace. This may end in madness and they may become the devil's contemplatives not God's.

Hence the emphasis on the necessity of a good spiritual director (not an easy thing to find these days) and the careful listing of the signs whereby a man may know if he is called to this work. The work is not selfish, the practice of it helps the living although you do not know how, and relieves the souls in purgatory. It is important to note that it can be carried on during the ordinary actions of daily life. "For in this unquestioning consideration of your bare being united with God, as I was telling you, you will do all that you do, eat, drink, sleep, wake" and all the other actions of daily life *Letter of Private Direction 5*. Ultimately the perfect disciple of Our Lord, with all self-will utterly destroyed, and his will in perfect accord with God's will (and this accord is perfect love) "will offer up his spirit to God in this spiritual work not only for those He loves but for all men in general as Christ offered up His body on the cross".

The Cloud of Unknowing was addressed to a young man aged 20 who had been a lay brother ("a servant of His special servants") and had been called by God to become a hermit.

Many people think that *The Letter of Private Direction* was written to the same person to clear up questions he had raised about *The Cloud*. But this does not seem to me to be the case, unless the recipient's nature had altered very much between the two letters. The whole tone and intellectual level of the letter is different. In *The Cloud* our author does not give his quotations in Latin, in *The Letter of Private Direction* he does, and does not always translate them. The teachings of the former are plain and easy to follow whereas those of the latter are more metaphysical and difficult and seem to be directed to a man on a higher intellectual plane than the man to whom *The Cloud* is addressed. In *The Cloud* the author, always humble, puts himself on the same level as the recipient. For instance he says (chapter 35) "I am far from attaining to it myself therefore I pray you to help me and act both for yourself and for me"; and again (chapter 73) "You may be Aaron working continually thereon for yourself and for me, and since we are both called by God to this work I beg you for God's love fulfil in your part what is lacking in mine".

In the latter he continually attacks the spiritual pride and self-will of the recipient as in chapter 7; "You set limits to your humility when you will not implement the advice of your spiritual director unless your mind considers it the thing to do"; and again when the disciples resented the loss of our Lord's bodily presence (chapter 13) he adds; "As you do to some extent and in a way resent giving up your speculative meditation and abstruse, clever reasoning". Our author, too, set out to undermine his spiritual pride by pointing out to him (chapter 8) that he had to lead him to the work by degrees "on account his inexperience and spiritual immaturity". Furthermore he says in chapter 7; "I mean to become your spiritual director": whereas he must by then have been spiritual director of the recipient of *The Cloud* for some time. In *The Cloud* our author cites Dionysius as his chief source and he quotes St. Gregory the Great, St. Augustine and St. Bernard, showing, as one would expect, a general knowledge of the Church Fathers. He follows Thomas Aquinas in his teaching about grace. He makes much use of Richard of St. Victor of whose "Benjamin Minor" he made a précis. He also seems to have used Guigo II's *Scala Claustralium*. Much of the teaching is very similar to that of *De Adhaerendo Deo,* attributed to Albert the Great (died 1284) but in its present form of a later date. But this may well be due to two separate writers following the same path and not to one influencing the other.

His own influence does not evolve outside the contemplative orders until modern times although we find an echo of his work in Vaughan the Silurist:

> There is in God—some say
> a deep but dazzling darkness; as men here
> say it is late and dusky, because they
> see not all clear.
> O for that night when I in Him
> Might live invisible and dim.

Vaughan was a fellow countryman and contemporary of Fr. Augustine Baker and may have discovered *The Cloud* through him.

In modern times *The Cloud* has had a considerable influence on T. S. Eliot particularly in the *Four Quartets* where we come on such lines as, "I said to my soul be still and let the darkness come upon you which shall be the darkness of God". And again: "In order to arrive at what you are not you must go through the way in which you are not". But the most surprising similarity is between the teaching of the Cloud and that of St. John of the Cross (who lived in Spain 1542–1591). It is most improbable that St. John ever saw a copy of *The Cloud*. This is a case of two men basing their work on the same sources and coming to the same conclusion. *The Cloud* has been hailed as a bridge between East and West, its teaching being compared to the Avesta, the sufis and to Buddhism especially Zen Buddhism, and the short prayer that *The Cloud* advocates being equated to the Buddhist mantra. But this is only due to the fact, to use St Augustine's metaphor of a wheel in which God is the hub and men the spokes, the nearer they come to the hub the closer they get to each other. For *The Cloud* is firmly founded on Christianity and the teaching of the Catholic Church. It is interesting to note that much of the teaching of modern psychology is similar to that of *The Cloud*. H. Benson praises the methods of *The Cloud's* author in his *Relaxation Response,* and Franze Wohrer shows how close the teaching of the German psychologist Carl Albrecht is to that of *The Cloud*.[1]

It is difficult in a modernisation neither to follow the text so exactly that it is virtually not modernised at all and is difficult to read and understand, (which happens amongst the earlier modernisations) nor to be so free with the text that the result is not so much a modernisaton as a paraphrase, and the reader loses the sensitivity of the author as well as the subtler nuances of the text (as happens in some recent versions).

I have followed Phyllis Hodgson's text in the Early English Text Society series except in a few instances when I have preferred alternative readings of other manuscripts as being more intelligible. I have included also the last paragraph of *The Letter of Private Direction* which Phyllis Hodgson completely ignores although it occurs in many manuscripts including the beautifully written Cambridge University Library I1 VI 31 one of the earliest manuscripts of *The Letter of Private Direction*. Without this paragraph *The Letter* has no proper ending. It would seem the last page must have been lost in one of the archetypal manuscripts. *The Letter of Private Direction* is not divided into chapters in the manuscripts. I have followed Dom Justin McCann's

---

[1] The Medieval Mystical Tradition in England (Dartington 1984)

chapter divisions except between chapters 12 and 13 which he divides in the middle of a paragraph.

Before ending the introduction I would like to emphasise the author's warning that in order to understand *The Cloud of Unknowing* one must read it carefully right through, and better still, read it more than once; and to repeat the sentence in *The Cloud* which most of all gives comfort to us who know only too well how far we have fallen short of that for which we have striven: "God with His merciful eyes does not regard what you are or what you have been but what you would be".

THE CLOUD OF UNKNOWING

Here begins a book of contemplation which is called "The Cloud of Unknowing" in which the soul is united with God.

Here begins the prayer of the Prologue.

God, to whom all hearts are open and the whole will speaks, and from whom no secret is hidden, I beg you so to clense the intention of my heart with the ineffable gift of your grace that I may perfectly love you, and worthily praise you.

Here begins the Prologue.

In the name of the Father, and of the Son, and of the Holy Spirit, I order and beg you, with as much power and strength as the restraining force of love allows, whoever you are who have this book in your possession whether as owner, or as custodian, or through carrying it as a messenger, or through borrowing it, that, as far as it lies in your power and discretion, you neither read nor write it out, nor speak of it, nor permit it to be read, written, or spoken about to anyone or by anyone except such a person (as you believe) who, with a true will and undeviating purpose intends to be a perfect follower of Christ, not only in his daily life, but in the highest degree of contemplative living that it is possible for a perfect soul, still in this mortal body to reach by grace in the present life: and to this end does all in his power, and, (as you believe) has done so for a long time to make himself capable of contemplative living by his virtuous conduct in daily life. Otherwise the book is not for him. Furthermore, I order and beg you, by the power of love, that if such a person reads it, or writes it out, or speaks of it or hears it read or spoken of, you order him, as I do you, to take time to read it, or write it out or hear it right through. Otherwise there may be something at the beginning, or in the middle of it which is left hanging in the air and not fully explained where it stands. But, if it is not explained there, it will be soon after, or by the end. So if anyone saw one part and not the other, he might easily be lead into error.

Therefore, that you may shun this, both in yourself and in anyone else, I pray you, for love's sake, to do as I tell you.

As for worldly chatterers, who freely praise and blame themselves and others, scandal-mongers, tale-bearers, gossips and all kinds of carping critics, I should not care at all if they never saw this book. For it was never my intention to write such a book for them and therefore I should rather that they did not meddle with it, neither these, nor those acting purely out of curiosity, whether men of letters or illiterates. Yes, even if they are very good men in their daily life, there is nothing in this for them.

The case is different for those men who, although in outward appearance they lead a life of action, nevertheless, by inward stirrings of the secret Spirit of God, whose purposes for us are hidden, are brought by grace to be partakers in the highest point of the contemplative act, not continually, as is the case with true comtemplatives, but now and then. If such men should see it they should, by God's grace, be greatly comforted by it.

This book is divided into seventy-five chapters and the last chapter of all gives certain signs by which a soul may truly determine whether he is called by God to practise this work or not.

THE CLOUD OF UNKNOWING

Chapter 75: Of some sure indications whereby a man may verify whether he is called by God to this work.

Here ends the Table of Chapters.

S piritual friend in God, I pray and beseech you that you have an earnest regard to the progress and manner of your vocation and thank God from the bottom of your heart so that through the help of His grace you may stand firm in that state, degree and form of living that you have whole-heartedly embraced in spite of all the subtle attacks of your bodily and spiritual enemies, and win to the crown of eternal life.

THE FIRST CHAPTER

Of the four degrees of Christian life, and the progress in his vocation of the man for whom this book was written

Spiritual friend, you must fully understand that I find, in my rough and ready opinion, four degrees and forms of Christian living. These are: Ordinary, Special, Singular and Perfect. Three of these may be begun and ended in this life. The fourth may, by the Grace of God, be begun here, but will last for ever without end in the bliss of Heaven. And even as you see them here set out in order one after another, first Ordinary, then Special, after that Singular, and finally Perfect, even so I think in the same order and in the same progression Our Lord has called and led you to Him through the desire of your heart.

For first, as you are well aware, you were leading the ordinary course of Christian life in company with your friends in the world. It seems to me that the everlasting love of the Godhead through which he made you and fashioned you when you were nothing, then bought you at the price of

His precious blood when you were lost in Adam, would not allow you to be so far away from Him in your manner and style of living: and so of His great grace he kindled your desire, and fastened through it a leash of longing, and with this He led you into a more special manner and style of living. This was so as to be a servant of His special servants, where you might learn to live more specifically and more spiritually in His service than you did, or could do in your ordinary state of living before that.

And what now? For it seems for the love of His heart which He always had for you since you came into being, that He would not lightly leave you in this state. But what did He do? Do you not see how eagerly and graciously He has drawn you to the third manner and style of living which is Singular? In this solitary form and manner of living you must learn to lift up the foot of your love and step towards that state and degree of living that is Perfect and is the last State of all.

THE SECOND CHAPTER

A short call to humility and to the teaching of this book

Look up now, weak wretch, and see what you are. What are you? What have you done to deserve to be called in this manner by our Lord? What a wretched heart is that, weary and sleeping in sloth, that is not awakened by the pull of His love and the voice of His calling! Wretch, beware of your enemy at this time, and do not hold yourself to be holier and better because of the worthiness of your vocation, and for the singular form of life you are living; but the more wretched and cursed unless you do all that is in you by grace and counsel to live in accordance with your vocation. So you should be more humble and loving to your spiritual spouse, since He that is God Almighty, King of Kings, Lord of Lords, is willing to humble Himself so low for you, and out

10

of all the flock of His sheep so graciously to select you to be one of His chosen, and then to set you in the field of pasture where you may be fed with the sweetness of His love as a foretaste of your heritage—the Kingdom of Heaven.

Act fast then, I pray you. Look forward now, and never mind what is behind; and see what you are lacking and not what you have, for that is the quickest way to get and keep humility. Your whole life now should always stand fast in desire if you are to advance in the state of perfection. This desire ought always to be generated in your will by the hand of Almighty God, and with your consent. But one thing I emphasise: He is a jealous lover who will not permit any rival and has no wish to work in your will unless He is alone with you by Himself. He wants no-one to help, but only you yourself. He only wants you to look at Him and leave Him alone. And you must guard the windows and doors against flies[1] and enemies who are attacking, and if you are willing to do this, you have but humbly to call upon Him with prayer and He will quickly help you. Call upon Him, then, and let us see how you fare. He is quite ready and only waits for you.

But what should you do, and how should you call upon Him?

THE THIRD CHAPTER

How the teaching of this book shall be carried out and that its value is beyond all other works

Lift up your heart to God in a humble stirring of love, and direct it to God Himself, and not to any of the good things He provides. And see to it that you have no wish to think on anything but God himself, so that nothing engages your mind or your will except Him. And do your best to forget all

---

[1] Flies: see Eccles. X. 1.

the created things that God ever made and all their works, so that your mind and your desire is not directed towards, nor reaching out for any of them, either in a general way or to a special object, but let them be, and take no heed of them. This is the work of the soul which most pleases God. All saints and angels take joy in this work and hasten to help it with all their might. All fiends are furious when you act like this, and try to frustrate it in every way they can. All men living on earth are wonderfully helped by this work, you do not know how. The souls in Purgatory are eased of their pain because of this work, and you yourself are cleansed and made virtuous by this, more than by any other work. Yet it is the easiest work of all, and soonest accomplished when the soul is helped by grace in its conscious longing, otherwise it is hard, and a miracle if you can do it. Do not let up then, but labour at it until you feel longing. For the first time you do it you find only darkness, and, as it were, a cloud of unknowing. You do not know what it is save that you feel in your will a pure aspiration towards God. This darkness and this cloud is, whatever you do, between you and your God, and prevents you from seeing Him clearly by the light of rational understanding, or feeling the sweetness of His love in your affection. And therefore prepare yourself to remain in this darkness as long as you can, evermore crying out to Him whom you love. For if ever you shall see Him or feel Him as far as you can here, it must always be in this cloud and in this darkness. If you will diligently labour as I bid you, I trust of His mercy that you may attain this.

THE FOURTH CHAPTER

Of the shortness of this work, and how it cannot be achieved by speculation of the mind, or by imagination

But that you should not go wrong in this work and think that it is something else than it is, I will tell you a little more of what I think about it. The work does not require much time before it is truly done, as some men think, but it is the shortest work of all that a man can imagine. It is neither longer nor shorter than an atom which is defined by true philosophers in the science of astronomy as the very smallest division of time, and it is so short, that from its shortness it is indivisible and almost incomprehensible. This is the time of which it is written: "You will be asked how you spent all the time that has been given to you", and it is reasonable that you should give account of it, for it is neither longer nor shorter but the same length as a single impulse which lies within the principal working power of your soul, that is to say, your will. For exactly the same number of wishes and desires—no more, no less—can be, and are in your will in one hour as there are atoms in an hour. If you were reformed by grace to the first state of man's soul as it was before sin came, you would always be, by the help of that grace, master of that impulse or these impulses; so that none went astray, but all would reach to that which is most desirable of all and the highest thing that we can will—that is God.

He is apt to our souls by the measuring of His Godhead, and our souls are apt to Him by the worthiness of our creation in His image and likeness.

He Himself alone and no-one but He is sufficient to fill to the full, and much more, the will and desires of our soul; and our soul by virtue of His reforming grace is made able fully to understand the whole of Him by love who is incomprehensible to all created knowing powers such as angels, and man's soul—I mean by their knowing, not by their loving, and therefore I call them in this case "knowing powers". All reasonable creatures, angels and men, have in them, each one individually, one principal working power which is called knowing power, and another principal working power which is called loving power. To the first of these, which is a knowing power, God who is the maker of them is forever incomprehensible. But to the second, which

13

is a loving power, in each one differently He is comprehensible to the full. Insomuch that one loving soul alone by itself, by virtue of love, can comprehend in itself Him who is able to fill full—and much more without comparison— all souls and angels that ever may be and this is a marvellous miracle of love that will never end. Forever He shall do it and never shall He cease from doing it. See this who by grace may see it, for the feeling of this is endless bliss and the contrary is endless pain.

Therefore, anyone who is so reformed by grace as to continue to guard the impulses of the will—as by nature he can never be without these impulses—should never in this life be without some taste of the endless sweetness and in the bliss of Heaven without the full food. Therefore, no wonder that I incite you to this work. This is the work, as you will hear later, in which man would have continued if he had not sinned; and it was for this work that man was made, and everything was made for man to help Him and further Him in it, and by this work man will be restored again.

Through failure in this work a man falls deeper and deeper into sin, and further and further from God, and by taking heed and continually working at this work alone, without anything else, man evermore rises higher and higher above sin and nearer and nearer to God. So take good care of time, how you spend it. For nothing is more precious than time. In one short moment of time, short as it is, heaven may be won or lost. This is a token that time is precious: God, who is the giver of time never gives two times together, but one after another. And He does this because He will not reverse the order or the appointed course of His creation. For time is made for man, not man for time. Therefore, God, who rules nature will not, in the giving of time, outstrip the natural impulse in man's soul which accords exactly with one time only; so that man, when he gives his account of the spending of time before God on Judgement Day, will not be able to excuse himself by saying: "You gave me two times at once, and I have but one impulse at a time".

But sorrowfully you now say: "What shall I do? And if this that you are saying is true, how shall I give account of each moment of time separately, I who am now twenty-four years of age and who up to this day never paid any attention to time? If I should now amend it, you know well, as is shown by what you have written before, that it is impossible for me, in the course of nature or through common grace to guard or to give satisfaction for any more moments of time than those that are to come. Yes, and what is more, I know from actual experience, that in time to come, through my very great fraility and slowness of spirit I shall in no way be able to control more than one impulse in a hundred, so that I am utterly trapped by these reasonings. Help me now, for the love of Jesus".

You have spoken very truly when you said: "For the love of Jesus". For in the love of Jesus shall be your help. Love is such a power that it makes everything shared. Therefore love Jesus, and everything that He has is yours. He, through his Godhead, is maker and giver of time. He, through His manhood is the true keeper of time. And He, through His Godhead and manhood together is in very truth judge, and the one who demands account of the spending of time. Bind yourself to Him then, by love and by belief. Then, by virtue of this knot, you will become partners with Him and with all who are bound to Him by love, that is to say with Our Lady Saint Mary who was full of grace in all the keeping of time, with the angels in heaven who can never lose time, and with the saints in heaven and on earth who, by the grace of Jesus keep time in perfect justice by virtue of their love.

Look! Here lies comfort; see clearly what it means and get some profit from it. But one thing I warn you about above all else. I cannot see that anyone can truly claim fellowship with Jesus and His righteous mother, His exalted angels and His saints unless he is such a man as does all that is in him, with the help of grace, to value time, so that he may be seen for his part to bring some profit, little though it is, to the community; as each of them does in his part.

Therefore, give attention to the work, and the marvellous way it works within your soul. For if it is truly conceived it is nothing else but a sudden and, as it were, unheralded impulse speedily springing up to God like a spark from a coal and it is marvellous the number of impulses that can be formed in the course of one hour in a soul that is disposed to this work. Moreover, in one impulse among all these, a soul may have suddenly and perfectly forgotten all created things. But immediately after each impulse, owing to the corruption of the flesh, the soul falls down again into some thought or into some deed done or undone. But what of it? For straight afterwards it rises again as suddenly as it did before.

From this, men can quickly understand the manner of this working and know that it is far away from any delusion, false imagination or fanciful opinon. These are caused, not by such a devout and humble blind impulse of love, but by a proud fantastical and imaginative mind. Such a proud fantastical intellect must always be borne down and stoutly trampled underfoot if this work is truly to be understood in purity of spirit. Whoever hears of this work either by reading about it or through someone speaking of it, and thinks that he can and ought to come to it by labour of his intellect (and therefore sits and racks his brains how this can be), and in this speculation strains his imagination perhaps against the course of nature, and feigns a manner of working which is neither physical or spiritual; truly this man, whoever he may be, is perilously deceived. So much so that unless God in His great goodness works His merciful miracle and makes him soon leave off this work and humble himself to accept the counsel of the experienced, he will either fall into fits of madness or else into other great dangers in the form of spiritual sins and the devil's deceits; through which he may easily lose both life and soul for all eternity.

Therefore, for the love of God, be wary in this work, and do not strain your intellect or your imagination in any way. For I tell you truly, you cannot reach your goal by labouring with them. Therefore leave them alone and do not work with them.

Do not think, because I call it darkness or a cloud, that it is any cloud that is congealed from the vapours that float in the air, or that it is the sort of darkness that is in your house at night when the candle is out. For such darkness and such a cloud you may imagine by the working of your mind to be before your eyes on the brightest day of summer; and on the contrary, in the darkest night of winter you may imagine a clear shining light. Let such falsehoods alone. I do not mean this when I say darkness; I mean a lack of knowledge. For all that you do not know or that you have forgotten is dark to you, as you do not see it with your spiritual eye; and for this reason it is not called a cloud of the air, but a cloud of unknowing that is between you and your God.

THE FIFTH CHAPTER

That when the work is being carried on, all created things that ever have been, are now, or ever shall be, and all the works of these created things, must be hidden under the cloud of forgetting

If you shall ever come to the cloud and stay and work in it as I bid you, it is necessary, even as the cloud of unknowing is above you between you and your God, in the same way to put a cloud of forgetting between you and all created things that have ever been made. You think, perhaps, that you are very far from God because that cloud of unknowing is between you and Him. But certainly, if it is properly understood, you are further from Him when you have no cloud of forgetting between you and all created things that have been made. When I use these words I always mean not only the created things themselves, but also the works and state of these same created things. I do not except any created thing at all, whether it is physical or spiritual, nor any state or work of any created thing, whether good or evil. But, to be brief, all should be hidden under the cloud of forgetting.

For though it is sometimes very profitable to think of certain states and deeds of some selected created things, in this work it profits little or not at all. This is because remembrance and thinking of any created thing that God ever made, or indeed of any of their acts, is a kind of spiritual light, and the eyes of your soul are attracted to it, and even fixed upon it as the eye of an archer is on the target at which he is shooting. And I tell you one thing, that all about which you are thinking is above you for the time being, and between you and your God. And insomuch as there is anything in your mind except God, by that much you are further from God. Yes! And if one can say so without discourtesy and disrespect, it profits little or nothing to think of the kindness and worthiness of God, Our Lady or the saints and angels in heaven, or even of the joys of heaven. I mean with a special attention to them as though you would, by that attention feed and increase your purpose. I believe it would not in any way help in this case and in this work; although it is good to think of the kindnesses of God and love and praise Him for them, yet it is far better to think of the simple being of God and love and praise Him for Himself.

THE SIXTH CHAPTER

A short summary of the teaching of this book by means of question and answer

But now you ask me a question and say: "How shall I think of God Himself and what is He?" And to this question I can only answer: "I never know"—for by your question you have brought me into the same darkness and into that same cloud of unknowing that I wish you were in yourself. A man, through grace, may have full knowledge of all other created things and all their works—yes, and if the works of God too—and be well able to think about them. But of God Himself no-one can think. Therefore I leave alone all those things about which I can think, and choose for my love that about which I cannot think, because He may well be loved but not thought about. By love He can be reached and held, but by thought never. And therefore, although it is sometimes good to think of the kindness and worthiness of God in particular, and although it is enlightening and a part of contemplation; nevertheless in this work it must be cast down and covered with a cloud of forgetting, and you must step above it resolutely, but with an eager longing and with a devout and pleasing impulse of pure love, and endeavour to pierce that darkness above you. You must smite upon that thick cloud of unknowing with a sharp dart of longing love, and not leave it whatever happens.

THE SEVENTH CHAPTER

How a man engaged in this work must set himself against all thoughts, especially those that spring from his own speculation, learning and natural intelligence

If any thought rises and will always push in above you, between you and the darkness and ask you: "What are you

19

seeking and what would you have?", answer that it is God that you would have, "Him I covet and seek, and nothing else but Him". And if it should ask you: "What is that God?", say that it is the God who made you, who redeemed you, and graciously called you to His love, and that He is beyond your understanding; and therefore say: "Get you down again" and quickly tread it down with an impulse of love, although it may seem to you very holy and you think it would help you to seek God.

For perhaps the thought will bring to your mind various beautiful and wonderful instances of God's kindness, and say that He is most sweet and most loving, most gracious and most merciful. And if you listen to it there is nothing it wants more. For in the end it will chatter ever more and more until it brings you down to remembrance of the Passion. And there it will let you see the wonderful kindness of God. If you listen to it, it wants nothing better. For soon after that it will lead you to see your old wretched life, and perhaps in seeing and thinking of this will bring to your mind some place where you formerly lived, so that at last, before you realise it, you will be led astray you never know where. The cause of this straying is that you listened to this thought in the first place, answered it, received it and let it alone.

Yet what it said was both good and holy. Yes, so holy that any man or woman who thinks to come to contemplation without any such sweet meditation on their wretchedness, the Passion, and the kindness, great goodness and worthiness of God coming first, certainly will err and fail in their purpose.

And yet it is necessary for a man or woman who has for a long time used these meditations nevertheless to leave them, and to put them and hold them far down under the cloud of forgetting, if he is ever to pierce the cloud of unknowing between him and his God. Therefore at the time when you determine to undertake this work, and feel by grace that you are called by God, lift up your heart to Him with a simple impulse of love, and attend to God that made you, redeemed you and has graciously called you to this work.

And have no other thought of God, and not even these, unless you desire it, for a simple impulse directed towards God is wholly sufficient, without any other grounds than God Himself.

And if your are eager to have this impulse wrapped up and folded in one word so that you may have a better hold on it, take only a little word of one syllable, for this is better than two. For the shorter it is, the better it accords with the work of the spirit. A suitable word is the word "God" or the word "Love". Choose which you will, or another word as you wish, any that you like best, of one syllable. Fasten the word on your heart so it never leaves it whatever happens. This word shall be your shield and your sword whether you ride out in peace or war. With this word you shall beat upon this cloud and this darkness above you. With this word you shall smite down every kind of thought under the cloud of forgetting; if any thought presses upon you and asks you what you would have, give it no other answer than this one word. And if it offers you of its great scholarship to expound that word and tell you its significance, say to it that you will have the word whole, not broken, nor undone, and if you hold fast to this purpose it will certainly not stay long. And why?—because you will not let it feed on such sweet meditation as we touched on before.

THE EIGHTH CHAPTER

A sound statement of certain doubts that may arise in the course of this work, by means of question and answer, in regard to the destroying of a man's own speculation arising from learning and natural intelligence, and to distinguishing the stages and parts of active and contemplative life

But now you ask me: "What is this thought that presses upon me in this work, and is it good or evil?" "If it is evil", you say, "I marvel that it will increase a man's devotion so much. For sometimes it seems to me that it is a great comfort to listen to its tales. It will sometimes, I think, make me weep heartily for pity at the Passion of Christ, and sometimes for my own wretchedness and for many other reasons that I think are very holy and have done me such good. Therefore I think that it could not in any way be evil. And if it is good, and moreover, with its sweet tales, benefits so much, I greatly marvel why it is that you bid me put it deep down under the cloud of forgetting".

I certainly think that this is a well propounded question and intend to answer it as best I can, though inadequately, First, when you ask me what it is that presses so hard upon you in this work, and offers to help you in it, I say that it is a sharp and clear impression of your natural intelligence imprinted on your reason within your soul. And when you ask me about it, whether it is good or evil, I say that it must always be good by nature, because it is a ray of the likeness of God. But the use of this thought may be both good and evil. Good when it is revealed by grace to see your wretchedness, the Passion, and the kindness and wonderful works of God in His creations, physical and spiritual—then it is no wonder that it increases your devotion as much as you say it does. But the use is evil when it is swollen up with pride and with the speculations springing from much scholarship and

22

book-learning, as is the case with clerics; with leads them to seek to be considered not humble scholars and masters of divinity and devotion, but proud scholars of the devil, and masters of vanity and falsehood. And in other men and women, whether they are religious or secular, the use and working of natural intelligence is evil when it is swollen up with pride and speculative learning in the things of this world, and with sensual ideas for coveting worldly honours and gaining riches and vane pleasures and flattery of others.

Next you ask why you should put it down under the cloud of forgetting, since it is good in its nature, and when used well does your mind good and increases your devotion so much. In answer to that I say that you must clearly understand that there are two kinds of life in Holy Church. The one is the active life, the other the contemplative life. The active life is the lower, the contemplative life the higher. Active life has two degrees, a higher and a lower. The contemplative life, too, has two degrees, a lower and a higher. These two lives are so coupled together that, although they are different in some parts, yet neither can be lived without some part of the other; because that which is the higher part of the active life is the same as the lower part of the contemplative life. So a man cannot be fully active unless he is in part contemplative, nor fully contemplative (at least in this life) unless he is, in part, active. The state of the active life is such that it both begins and ends in this life; but the contemplative life, although it begins in this life, shall last for ever. For the part that Mary chose shall never be taken away. The active life is anxious and harassed about many things, but the contemplative sits in peace with the one thing only.

The lower part of the active life consists of good, honest bodily work of mercy and charity. The higher part of the active life and the lower part of the contemplative life lies in good spiritual meditations and earnest considerations of a man's own wretchedness with sorrow and contrition of the

Passion of Christ and His servants with pity and compassion, and of the wonderful gifts; kindness and the works of God in all His creation, physical and spiritual, with thanksgiving and praise. But the higher part of contemplation (as it may be experienced in this life), is suspended wholly in this darkness and in this cloud of unknowing, with a loving impulse and sightless vision towards the simple being of God Himself alone.

In the lower part of the active life a man is outside himself and beneath himself. In the higher part of the active life and the lower part of the contemplative life a man is within himself and level with himself. In the higher part of the contemplative life a man is above himself and under God. He is above himself because he is determined to win by grace to that place where he cannot come by nature—that is to say, to knit himself to God in spirit, in union of love and accordance of will.

Just as it is impossible as far as man's understanding goes for a man to come to the higher part of active life unless he relinquishes for a time the lower part, so it is that a man cannot come to the higher part of contemplation unless he relinquishes for a time the lower part. And as it is wrong, and would greatly hinder a man that sat in meditation to consider at that time his outward bodily works which he had done or should do, although they were ever such holy works in themselves; certainly it is equally unsuitable and would be as much of a hindrance to a man who should be working in this darkness and in this cloud of unknowing with an eager impulse of love for God Himself, if he should let any thought or meditation about God's wonderful gifts, kindness and works in any of His created things, physical or spiritual, rise up and push in between him and his God; even though they were ever such holy thoughts and so pleasant and so comforting.

It is for this reason I bid you put down such a sharp subtle thought and cover it with a thick cloud of forgetting although it be ever so holy and promises it will give you very great help in your purpose: because love may reach to God in this life, but not knowledge. As long as our soul is united with this mortal body, always the sharpness of our understanding in the contemplation of all spiritual matters, but especially of God, is mixed with some kind of fantasy through which our work would be unclean; and but for a miracle, it would lead us into much error.

THE NINTH CHAPTER

That during this work, remembrance of the holiest creature that God ever made, hinders more than it helps

Therefore the keen impulse of your understanding that will always press down upon you when you set yourself to this unseeable work, must always be borne down; for if you do not bear it down it will bear you down, to such an extent that when you think you are best established in this darkness, and that nothing is in your mind but only God, if you examine it truly you will find that your mind is not occupied in this darkness but in a clear vision of something lower than God. And if this is so, it is certain that this thing is above you for the time being, and between you and your God. Therefore, determine to put down such clear visions however holy and pleasant they may be. For I can tell you one thing, this blind impulse of love of God for Himself, and this secret love beating upon the cloud of unknowing, is more profitable in helping your soul, more worthwhile in itself, and more pleasing to God and to all the saints and angels in heaven; yes, and more helpful both bodily and spiritually to your friends living and dead. It is better for you to have this, and feel it in your spiritual disposition, than to have the eyes of your soul opened in contemplation, either seeing all the angels or saints in heaven, or hearing all the mirth and melody that those in bliss enjoy.

You should not wonder at this; for if you could once see it as clearly as you can by grace touch it and feel it in this life, you would agree with what I say. But you can be certain that a man will never have that clear sight here in this life. But men can have the feeling of it by grace when God grants it. And therefore lift up your love to that cloud; or to speak more truly, let God draw your love up to that cloud, and through the help of His grace, forget everything else. Since a simple remembrance of anything less than God pushing against your will and your intellect puts you further from Him than you would be if it were not there, and hinders you, and makes you so much the less able to feel by experience the fruit of His love; how much more then do you think a remembrance knowingly and deliberately brought into your mind hinders you in that purpose?

And since the remembrance of any special saint, or any pure spiritual thing would hinder you so much, how much more, then, do you think the remembrance of any man living this wretched life, or of any kind of bodily or worldly thing will hinder and obstruct you in this work?

I do not say the simple unexpected thought of any good and pure spiritual matter under God pressing against your will and your intelligence, or else purposely brought up with deliberation for increasing your devotion, although it hinders you in this sort of work, is therefore evil. No, God forbid that you should take it like that. But I do say that although it is good and holy, in this work it hinders more than it helps. I mean for the time being. For surely he that seeks God perfectly will not, in the end, be content to let himself rest in the remembrance of any angel or saint in heaven.

THE TENTH CHAPTER

*How a man should know when his thought is not sinful,
and, if sinful, when it is mortal and when venial*

But it is different in the case of the remembrance of any
living man or woman, or of any bodily or worldly thing
whatever. For a simple unexpected thought of any of these
things pressing upon your will and your intelligence,
although no sin is imputed to you (for it is the hurt of
original sin pressing against your powers, and you were
cleansed of this sin at baptism) nevertheless, if this sudden
impulse or thought is not soon struck down, your heart of
flesh, because of its fraility will as soon be attached by it to
some kind of gratification if the thing pleases you or has
pleased you before; or else to some kind of resentment, if it is
a thing that you think grieves you or has grieved you before.

This attachment may be a mortal sin in worldly-living
men and women who were in a state of mortal sin already;
but in you and in all others that have with a true intention
forsaken the world, and have pledged themselves, in any
form to devout living in Holy Church, whatever it may be
whether secretly or openly; and who therefore will be governed not by their own will and intelligence, but by the will
and counsel of their superiors whether they are religious or
secular, in all of you this gratification and resentment
attached to the heart of flesh is but a venial sin. This is
because your aspiration when you began to live in that state
of life in which you still persevere, was rooted and grounded
in God.

But if it happens that this gratification or this resentment
fastening on your heart of flesh is allowed to stay there
unreproved for so long that at last it is attached to your
spiritual heart, (that is your will) and that with your full
consent; then it is a mortal sin. This happens when you, or
any of those I speak about, wilfully bring into your mind the

27

remembrance of any living man or woman, or of any other bodily or worldly thing, to such an extent that if it is a thing that grieves you, ·or has grieved you before, there rises in you an angry passion, and an appetite for vengeance. This is called Wrath. Or if a cruel disdain and a sort of loathing for a person, with malevolent or reproving thoughts occurs, this is called Envy. Or if a weariness and lack of enthusiasm for any good occupation bodily or spiritual occurs, this is called Sloth.

And if it is a thing that pleases you or has pleased you before, and there arises in you an immediate delight in thinking about it whatever it is, to such an extent that you dwell on that thought and finally fasten your heart and will to it, and feed your heart of flesh with it so that during that time you think that you desire no other good fortune than always to live in such peace, and rest with the thing about which you were thinking. If this thought which you have conjured up or accepted when it was put to you, and on which you dwell with such delight is about the nobility of your nature, the pre-eminence of your learning, charm, rank, appearance or beauty, then it is Pride. If it is about any sort of worldly goods, riches, property, or what a man may have, or be master of, then it is Covetousness. If it is about dainty food and drink, or any of the pleasures of the palate, then it is Gluttony. If it is about the pleasures of love, or any kind of amorous dalliance, cajoling and flattering any living man or woman, or indeed yourself, then it is Lust.

THE ELEVENTH CHAPTER

That a man should recognise each thought and impulse for what it is, and always shun recklessness in venial sin

I do not say this because I believe that you, or any other such as I speak of, are guilty and burdened with any sins of this sort, but I wish you to attach importance to each thought and each impulse according to what it is; and I would have you work hard to destroy the first impulse and thought of those things which may lead you into sin. For I can tell you this, that he who does not attach importance to the first thought, and holds it of little account—although it is not imputed to him for sin—whoever he is, he will not avoid recklessness in venial sin.

Venial sin none can entirely avoid in this mortal life, but recklessness in venial sin should always be avoided by all followers of perfection. Otherwise I do not wonder that, as a result, they soon commit mortal sin.

THE TWELFTH CHAPTER

That by the power of this work not only is sin destroyed, but virtue gained

Therefore, if you would stand and not fall, never cease from your purpose, but beat continually upon the cloud of unknowing that lies between you and your God with the sharp dart of longing love. Do not allow yourself to think of anything lower than God, and do not leave the work whatever happens. For it is the only work that, by itself, destroys the ground and root of sin. However much you fast, however long you keep awake, however early you rise, however hard your bed and however rough your hair shirt; yes, and if it were lawful (which it is not), though you put out your eyes, cut out your tongue, stop up your ears and your nose ever so tightly, shear away your private parts, and afflict your body with all the pain you could devise; all this would help you not at all, for the impulse and uprising of sin will still be with you.

Yes, and still more, however much you weep in sorrow for your sins, or for the Passion of Christ, and however much you think of the joys of heaven, what will it do for you? Much good, certainly, much profit and much grace, yet in comparison with this blind impulse of love there is little that it does or can do, without this impulse. This, without anything else, was the best part which Mary chose. Without this, other things profit little or nothing. This not only destroys the ground and root of sin as far as can happen in this life, but also it gains virtue for if it is truly understood, all virtue should be truly and perfectly conceived, felt and comprehended in it, without any debasing of your purpose. However many virtues a man may have, without this they are all debased with some devious purposes, therefore they are imperfect. For virtue is nothing else but an ordered and controlled longing clearly directed to God for Himself. This is because God in Himself is the pure cause of all virtue; so much so that, if a man is stirred to any single virtue by any other cause mixed with Him, although He is the main cause, yet that virtue is imperfect. This can be seen if one or two virtues are taken to cover all the rest. These two may well be humility and charity, for whoever can get these two, clearly needs no more because he has all of them.

THE THIRTEENTH CHAPTER

What is the nature of humility, and when it is perfect and when imperfect

Now let us first look at the virtue of humility, how it is imperfect when it is caused by anything mixed with God although God is the main cause, and how it is perfect when it is caused by God alone. The first thing to know is what is humility in itself, if this matter is to be clearly seen and understood. And thereafter we may more truly understand what its cause is.

Humility in itself is nothing else than a man's true knowledge and feeling for himself as he is. For certainly anyone who might see and feel himself as he is would be very humble. There are two things which cause this humility;

they are these. First, the filth, wretchedness and weakness of a man into which he has fallen through sin, and which he must always feel in some degree as long as he lives, however holy he is. The other is the superabundant love and worthiness of God in Himself. At seeing this, all nature quakes, all clerks are fools and all saints and angels are blind, to such an extent that, but for the wisdom of His Godhead, in that He measures Himself to their sight in accordance with their capabilities in nature and grace, I cannot say what would happen to them.

The second cause is perfect because it will last forever. The first one is imperfect, for, not only will it fail at the end of this life, but it may often happen that a soul in this mortal body, through abundance of grace in multiplying its desire (as often and as long as God condescends to work it), will have suddenly and completely lost and forgotten all knowledge and feeling of its being, not considering whether it is holy or a sinner. Whether this happens often or seldom to a soul that is so disposed, I believe it will last for a very short time. During this time, a soul is made perfectly humble, for it knows and feels no cause except the main one. But always, when it knows and feels any other causes joining up with it, although God is the main cause, yet it is imperfect humility. Nonetheless, it is good, and we must always have it. God forbid that you take it in any other manner than that which I say.

THE FOURTEENTH CHAPTER

That without imperfect humility coming first, it is impossible for a sinner to come to the perfection of humility in this life

In spite of the fact that I call it imperfect humility, yet I would rather have a true knowledge and feeling of myself, wretch that I am, and I believe that it alone would get me the

31

perfect cause and virtue of humility sooner than if all the saints and angels in heaven and all the members of the Church living on earth, men and women, religious and secular of all degrees, were set together at one time to do nothing else but pray God for me that I should get perfect humility. Yes, for it is impossible for a sinner to get perfect humility or to keep it when he has got it, without imperfect humility.

Therefore toil and sweat as much as you can and may to get a true knowledge and feeling of yourself as the wretch that you are, and then I believe soon after that you will have a true knowledge and feeling of God as He is. Not as He is in Himself—for that no-one can know but Himself. Nor yet as you will know Him in heaven, both body and soul together, but as much as is possible and as He allows to be felt by a humble soul living in this mortal body.

Do not think that because I set out two kinds of humility, one perfect and the other imperfect, that I would have you therefore leave off working for the imperfect humility and induce you to go solely after the perfect. No, certainly not, for I do not believe you would ever accomplish that. But my purpose in doing as I do is to tell you and let you see that the excellence of this spiritual exercise is greater than that of all the others, bodily or spiritual, that a man can or may perform through grace; and how a secret love, put in cleanness of spirit upon this dark cloud of unknowing between you and your God, truly and perfectly contains in it the perfect virtue of humility without any special or clear view of anything less than God. I wish you to know what perfect humility is, to set it as a sign before the love of your heart, and to do so for yourself and for me; and I wish by this knowledge to make you more humble.

For I think that it often happens that lack of knowledge is the cause of much pride. Perhaps, if you did not know what perfect humility was, you would think when you had a little knowledge and feeling of this which I call imperfect humility, that you had nearly reached perfect humility; and so you would deceive yourself, and think that you were very humble when you were wrapped around with foul, stinking pride.

Therefore endeavour to work for perfect humility, for such is its nature that whoever has it will not sin while he has it, nor much thereafter.

THE FIFTEENTH CHAPTER

A short confutation of the error of those who say that there are no more perfect grounds for humility than remembrance of a man's own wretchedness

Believe firmly that there is such a perfect humility as I am speaking of, and that it may come through grace in this life. I say this in confutation of the error of those that say that there are no more perfect grounds for humility than those which are brought about by the memory of our wretchedness and our former sins.

I grant freely that for those like myself, who are, and have been used to commit besetting sins, it is most needful and helpful to be humbled by memory of our wretchedness and former sins until the time comes when that great rust of our sins is (for the most part) rubbed away, as our conscience and our director bear witness.

But for others who are to all intents and purposes innocent, who have never committed mortal sin with a stubborn will and full knowledge, but through weakness and ignorance, and who set themselves to be contemplatives—and to both of us, also, if our director and our conscience testify to our proper amendment through contrition, confession, and making full satisfaction after the laws and ordinance of Holy Church, and moreover, if we feel ourselves stirred and called by grace to be contemplatives—there is then another cause for humility. This is as far above the first as the life of

Our Lady Saint Mary is above that of the most sinful peni-
tent in Holy Church, or the life of Christ above that of any
other living man; or the life of an angel in heaven which
never felt nor shall feel weakness is above the life of the
weakest man in the world.

If there were no other perfect cause to make us humble but
the seeing and feeling of our wretchedness, I would like
those that say this to tell me the cause of humility in those
who never see nor feel, and shall never admit in themselves,
either wretchedness or the impulse of sin nor ever shall; as is
the case with Our Lord Jesus Christ, Our Lady Saint Mary
and all the saints and angels in heaven.

To this perfection and all others, Our Lord Jesus calls us in
the gospel where He bids us to be perfect by grace as He is by
nature.[1]

THE SIXTEENTH CHAPTER

*Through the good effects of this work, a sinner truly
converted and called to contemplation comes sooner to
perfection than by any other method, and by it he will
most quickly get forgiveness from God for his sins*

Do not let anyone think it presumptuous that he who is the
most wretched of sinners in this life dare take upon himself,
when he has made proper amendment, and after he has felt
drawn to that life which is called contemplative—with the
agreement of his director and his conscience—to proffer a
humble impulse of love to his God, secretly pressing upon
the cloud of unknowing between him and his God.

When Our Lord said to Mary, as representative of all
sinners that are called to the contemplative life: "Your sins
are forgiven you",[2] He did not say it on account of her
sorrow for the remembrance of her sins, nor for her humil-

[1] Matt. V. 48.
[2] Luke VII. 48.

34

ity in considering her wretchedness. Why did He, then? Truly because she loved much. So here men can see what a secret love may gain from Our Lord more than any other work that a man can think of.

I freely grant that she was full of sorrow and wept bitterly for her sins and was humbled by the memory of her wretchedness. Even so we, who have been wretched and habitual sinners all our lives, should have intense and wonderful sorrow for our sins, and be greatly humbled by the memory of our wretchedness. But how? Certainly as Mary did. Although she might not relieve her deep sorrow for her sins because they were with her all her life, wherever she went, like a burden bound together, and laid up very secretly in the depths of her heart in such a way as never to be forgotten; nevertheless, it may be said and is affirmed by scripture, that she had a much more heart-felt sorrow, more doleful desire and deeper sighs—and she languished more, yes nearly to death, for lack of love, although she had such a full measure of love, than ever she did for memory of her sins. And do not wonder at it, it is the condition of the true lover that the more he loves, the more he longs to love.

Yet she knew well, and felt in herself with sorrowful insight, that she was a wretch, foul beyond all others and that her sins had made a division between her and her God, whom she loved so much; and also that they were in a great part the cause of her languishing sickness for lack of love.

What was the result? Did she therefore come down from the height of her desire into the depths of her sinful life and search in the foul, stinking bog and dunghill of her sins, dredging them out with all the circumstances surrounding them; and did she sorrow and weep over each one separately? No, certainly she did not do this. Why? Because God let her know by His grace within her soul that she would never bring it about. For in doing so, she was more likely to have raised up in herself a capability to sin often than to gain by that method a full forgiveness of all her sins.

Therefore she hung up her love and her longing desire in this cloud of unknowing, and learnt to love that which she might not in this life see clearly by the light of her understanding in her mind, nor truly feel in the sweetness of love in her affection; so that she often had little real memory of whether she had been a sinner or not. Yes—and very often, I believe, she was so deeply affected by love of this Godhead that she took very little particular notice of the beauty of His precious and blessed body in which he sat, beautiful to see, speaking and preaching before her; nor of anything else, physical or spiritual. That that was so, the Gospel testifies.

THE SEVENTEENTH CHAPTER

The true contemplative does not care to involve himself in the affairs of active life, nor with what is done or spoken about him, nor even to answer his critics by making excuses for himself

It is written in the Gospel of St. Luke[1], that when Our Lord was in the house of Martha, all the time that Martha was very busy preparing His meal her sister Mary sat at His feet. While listening to His words, she did not notice how busy her sister was, although Martha's work was very good and very holy—for it was the first part of the active life; nor did she regard the perfection of His blessed body, nor His sweet voice and the words He spoke as a man, in spite of the fact that this was better and more holy—for it was the second part of the active life, and first part of the contemplative. She only paid regard to the highest wisdom of the Godhead wrapped up in the obscure words He spoke as a man, and this she looked on with all love of her heart; for she had no desire to move away for anything that she saw or heard spoken or done around her. She sat with her body quite still

[1] Luke X. 38–41.

and pressed upon that cloud of unknowing between her and her God with many sweet, secret and eager impulses of love.

I tell you this, that there was never yet any pure creature alive, nor ever shall be, so highly caught up in the contemplation and love of the Godhead that he had not always a high and wonderful cloud of unknowing between him and his God.

It was in this cloud that Mary was occupied with many an impulse of secret love. This was because it was the best and most holy part of contemplation that could be had in this life, and from this part she had no desire to move for anything. So that when her sister Martha complained to Our Lord about her, and told Him to order her sister to get up and help her so that she did not have to work and toil all by herself, Mary just sat still and did not utter a word in reply; she did not even frown at her sister, in spite of any complaint that Martha might make. No wonder; for she had other work to do that Martha did not know about, and therefore she had no time to listen to her, or answer her complaints.

You see, my friend, that these deeds, these words and these gestures that passed between Our Lord and the two sisters, are an example to all actives and all contemplatives that have been in Holy Church since that time, or shall be until the Day of Judgement. For by Mary is understood all contemplatives, for they should model their living on hers, and by Martha all actives, in the same manner, and for the self-same reason.

THE EIGHTEENTH CHAPTER

How even to-day all those who lead an active life complain about the contemplatives as Martha did about Mary. The complaints are due to ignorance

Just as Martha complained about Mary, her sister, so to this day actives complain about contemplatives. For if there is a man or woman in any company in the world, whether religious or secular, and I except none, and the man or woman (whichever it is) feels stirred by grace and counsel to forsake all outward business and set himself to live entirely the contemplative life in accordance with his knowledge and his conscience, and with the agreement of his director; then at once his brothers and sisters and all his close friends, and many others who do not know his impulses nor the manner of living that he is adopting, will set upon him with a great spirit of complaint and say sharply to him that what he is doing is no good. Further, they will quickly rake up many false tales, and true ones, too, of the downfall of men and women who have undertaken this sort of life in the past; and never a good tale of those who have persevered in it.

I agree that many fall and have fallen who had in appearance forsaken the world. Where they should have become God's servants and His contemplatives, because they would not govern themselves by true spiritual counsel they have become the devil's servants and his contemplatives; and they have turned into either hypocrites or heretics, or fallen into frenzies or other misfortunes, to the scandal of the whole Church. I am not going to talk about this at present for fear of disrupting our teaching. But later on, when God grants it, and there is need, we may see some of the conditions and the causes of their falling. Therefore, no more of them for the time being, but to get on with our subject.

THE NINETEENTH CHAPTER

A short defence of the author of this book for his teaching that all contemplatives should completely excuse all those living an active life for their complaining words and deeds

Some would think that I do little honour to Martha, that special saint, when I liken her words of complaint to her sister to the words of worldly men and theirs to hers. Truly I mean no disrespect, to her or to them. God forbid that I should, in this work, say anything that might be taken as reproving any of the servants of God in any way, and most of all His special saint.

I think that she had every excuse for her complaints, paying regard to the time and manner in which she said what she did. For she spoke without knowledge; and no wonder she did not know how Mary was occupied at the time, for I believe that before that she had heard little of such perfection. Also, she said it courteously and in a few words, and therefore she should always be held excused.

Therefore I think that those men and women who live in the world and lead an active life should be completely excused on account of their ignorance for the words of complaint which I touched on before, even though they say what they say very rudely. For just as Martha had little knowledge of what her sister Mary was doing when she complained of her to Our Lord, even so, in the same way, people nowadays know very little or nothing at all about what these young disciples of God intend when they withdraw from the business of the world and undertake to be God's special servants in holiness and righteousness of spirit. If they really knew, I dare say they would not act or speak as they do.

Therefore I think they should always be excused because they know of no better life than the one that they live themselves. What is more, when I think of the numerous faults I myself have committed in the past, both in word and deed, through lack of knowledge, I think then that if I would be forgiven by God for my faults through ignorance, I should always lovingly and sympathetically forgive other men's ignorant words and deeds. For most certainly otherwise I do not do to others as I would they did to me.[1]

THE TWENTIETH CHAPTER

How Almighty God will make a good answer for all those who are not willing to leave their business of loving Him in order to excuse themselves

I think that those who set out to be contemplatives should not only forgive those in active life their words of complaint, but also it seems to me that they should be so occupied with spiritual things that they should take very little notice, or none at all, of what men do or say about them. This is what Mary, the example for us all, did when Martha her sister complained to Our Lord. If we truly act like this Our Lord will do for us now what He then did for Mary.

And what did He do? Most certainly this. Our loving Lord Jesus Christ, from whom no secret is hidden, although all Martha wanted Him to do in His capacity as judge was to order Mary to get up and help her to serve Him; nevertheless since He perceived that Mary was fervently occupied in spirit with the love of His Godhead, courteously and reasonably as befitted Him He answered on behalf of her who would not leave off loving Him to make excuses for herself. And how did He answer? Certainly not as a judge, in which guise Martha appealed to Him, but as an advocate, rightly defending her who loved Him, and saying: "Martha, Martha—" (twice for emphasis He called her name for He

[1] Matt. VII. 12.

wished her to hear Him and take notice of His words)—
"Your are busy", He said, "and troubled about many
things". For those who live the active life must always be
busy and working at many various things which they need,
first for their own use and then for the deeds of mercy to
their fellow Christians as love demands. This He explained
to Martha so that He might let her understand that her
works were good and profitable to the health of her soul.
But that she might not therefore think that this was the best
work of all that anyone might do, He added: "But one thing
is necessary". What was this one thing? Most certainly that
God should be loved and praised for Himself alone, above all
other work, physical and spiritual that anyone can do. And
in order that Martha should not think that she could love
God and praise Him above all other business, physical and
spiritual, and at the same time be busy about the necessities
of life; therefore to make it clear to her that she could not
perfectly serve God in physical or spiritual business
together,—she could do it imperfectly, but not perfectly,—He went on to say that Mary had chosen the best
part, and it would never be taken away from her. That was
because the perfect impulse of love that begins here is equal
in all respects to that which will last forever in the bliss of
heaven. They are both the same.

THE TWENTY-FIRST CHAPTER

*A true explanation of the gospel words: "Mary has
chosen the best part"*

What is the meaning of "Mary has chosen the best part"?
Whenever "best" is set down and named, it asks for two
things before it—a good and a better, so that it may be the
best and the third in number.

But what are these three good things of which Mary chose
the best? They are not three kinds of living, for Holy Church

makes mention of only two: the active and the contemplative life. These two are secretly represented in the story in the gospel by the two sisters Martha and Mary. By Martha the active life, by Mary the contemplative. Without one of these two lives no man can be saved, and where there are no more than two, no man can choose the best.

Although there are but two forms of living, nevertheless in these two lives there are three parts, each better than the other. These three, each one separately, have been specially set in their places earlier in this book. For, as is stated earlier, the first part consists of good and honest bodily works of mercy and charity. This, as was said before, is the first degree of active life. The second part of these two lives lies in good spiritual meditation about a man's own wretchedness, the Passion of Christ and the joys of heaven. The first part is good, but the second part is better, for it is the second degree of the active life and the first degree of contemplative life. In this part, contemplative life and active life are coupled together in spiritual relationship and made sisters after the example of Martha and Mary. This high may an "active" come towards contemplation but no higher, except very seldom and by special grace. This low a contemplative may come towards an active life, but no lower, except very seldom and in great need.

The third part of these two lives hangs in this dark cloud of unknowing, with many a secret act of love directed to God alone. The first part is good, the second better and the third best of all. This is the "best part" which is Mary's. Therefore it must be clearly understood that Our Lord did not say: "Mary has chosen the best life", for there are only two lives, and no one can choose the best of two. But of these two lives He said: "Mary has chosen the best part, and this shall never be taken from her". The first part and the second, although they are both good and holy, yet they end with this life. For in the other life there will be no need, as now, to use works of mercy, nor to weep for our wretched-

ness nor for the Passion of Christ. For then shall no one
hunger or thirst as now, nor die from cold, nor be sick nor
homeless nor in prison nor need burial, for then no one shall
die. But the third part that Mary chose, let him choose who
is called by grace to choose; or to speak more truly, whoever
is chosen for it by God, let him eagerly incline to it, for that
shall never be taken away; for though it begins here, it will
last for ever.

Therefore let the voice of Our Lord cry to these "actives",
as if He now said on our behalf to them, as He did then on
Mary's behalf to Martha: "Martha, Martha"; "Actives,
actives! Make your lives as busy as you can in the first part
and the second, now in one, now in the other; and if you
have a strong desire and feel disposed to it, in both of them
bodily. And do not meddle with my contemplatives, for
you do not know what affects them. Let them sit here at rest
and indulge in the third and best part which is Mary's".

THE TWENTY-SECOND CHAPTER

*Of the wonderful love that Christ had for Mary as
representing all sinners truly converted and called to the
grace of conteimplation*

Sweet was the love between Our Lord and Mary Mag-
dalene. She had much love for Him, and He had much more
for her. For whoever would see completely all that happened between Him and her (not as idle gossip would tell it,
but as the gospel story witnesses, which can in no way be
untrue), would find that her heart was so set on loving Him
that nothing less than He would comfort her or keep her
heart from Him. This is the same Mary who when weeping
sought Him at the sepulchre, and would not be comforted
by angels. For when they spoke to her so sweetly and so
lovingly and said: "Do not weep, Mary, for Our Lord
whom you seek is risen, and you shall see Him alive in all His

beauty among His disciples in Galilee as He promised",[1] she would not leave off for them, because she thought that whoever sought the King of Angels Himself should not leave off for mere angels.

What else? Whoever looks carefully at the story in the gospel will find many wonderful instances of perfect love written about her as an example to us, and so much in accordance with the work of this book that they might have been set down and written for that very purpose—as indeed they were. Let him understand them who is able to. If anyone wants to study in the Gospel the wonderful and special love that Our Lord had for Mary as representative of all habitual sinners truly converted and called to the grace of contemplation, he will find that Our Lord would not allow any man or woman, not even her own sister, to speak a word against her without answering for her Himself. Still further, He even blamed Simon the leper in his own house because of the thoughts he had against her.[2] This was great love, this was surpassing love.

THE TWENTY-THIRD CHAPTER

How God will answer and provide for them in spirit, that on account of their occupation with His love have no desire to answer or provide for themselves

Indeed, if we eagerly conform our love and our way of life, as far as we can by grace and counsel, to the love and the way of life of Mary, there is no doubt that in the same way even to-day He will spiritually give answer for us in secret in the hearts of all those who either speak or think against us. I do not deny that there will always be some men that speak or think against us on some point as long as we live in this

[1] Matt. XXVIII. 1–7, John XX. 11–13.
[2] Luke VII. 36 ff.

troubled life, as they did against Mary. But I do say that we should pay no more heed to their words and their thinking, and no more leave off our secret spiritual work for their words and their thoughts, than she did,—I say then that if all is well with them that say and think so, the Lord will answer them spiritually, so that within a few days they will be ashamed of their words and their thoughts.

And, as God will answer for us in spirit, so He will stir up other men spiritually to give us the things that we need that belong to this life, like food and clothes and all other necessities, if he sees that we will not leave the work of loving Him to busy ourselves about them. I say this in contradiction of their error who say that it is not allowable for men to set themselves to serve God in contemplative life unless they have made sure beforehand of securing their bodily necessities. For they say: "God sends the cow, but not by the horn".[1] Truly they speak wrongfully of God as they well know. For trust steadfastly, you whoever you may be who truly turn from the world to God, that God will send you one of two things without you busying yourself about it—either abundance of necessities, or else strength of body and patience of spirit to endure your needs. What does it matter which a man has, for it is all one to true contemplatives? Whoever doubts this, either the devil is in his heart and robs him of belief, or else he is not yet truly turned to God as he should be,—whoever he is, and whatever ingenious and holy arguments he may bring against it.

Therefore you, who set out to be a contemplative as Mary was, must choose rather to be humbled by the wonderful transcendency and worthiness of God which is perfect, than by your own wretchedness which is imperfect. That is to say, see that your special consideration is more about worthiness of God than about your own wretchedness. For to them that are perfectly humbled nothing shall be wanting,

---

[1] A mediaeval proverb meaning God helps those who help themselves.

either physical or spiritual, for they have God in whom is all plenty; and he who has Him, as this book tells, needs nothing else in life.

THE TWENTY-FOURTH CHAPTER

What charity is in itself, and how it is subtly and perfectly contained in the work of this book

As has been said of humility, that it is truly and perfectly comprehended in this little blind love when it is beating upon the dark cloud of unknowing, all else put down and forgotten; so it must be understood of all other virtues, especially charity. For charity means nothing else but love of God for Himself above all creatures, and of men even as yourself for God's sake. It seems very certain that in this work, God is loved for Himself above all creatures. For as has been said before, the substance of this work is nothing else but a pure intention directed towards God for Himself. A pure intention I call it because in this work the perfect apprentice asks neither for release from pain nor increase of reward but, to put it shortly, for nothing but God Himself. He neither cares nor notices whether he is in pain or bliss, but only that the will of Him he loves is fulfilled; and so it is seen that in this work God is perfectly loved for Himself, and that above all creatures. For in this work, a perfect worker will not allow the thought of the holiest creature that God ever made to have a share with Him.

And that in contemplation the second and lower branch of charity to your fellow Christian is truly and perfectly fulfilled as is seen by the proof. For in this work a perfect worker has no special regard for any man for himself, whether he is a relation or stranger, friend or foe; for he sees all men alike as related to him and no man a stranger. All men seem to him to be his friends and none his foes,—so much so that he thinks that all those that give him pain and cause him trouble in this life are his full and special friends, and he is stirred to wish them as much good as he would to the closest friend that he has.

THE TWENTY-FIFTH CHAPTER

That while engaged in this work, the perfect soul has no special regard for any one man in this life

I do not say that in this work a man should have any special regard for anyone in this life whether he is friend or enemy, relation or stranger. Such a thing is impossible if the work is to be perfectly carried out, as it is when all things less than God have been entirely forgotten, as happens in this work. But I do say that he will be made so virtuous and loving by reason of this work that afterwards, when he brings himself down to associate with and pray for his fellow Christians, his will shall have as much regard for his enemy as for his friend, for a stranger as for a relative. Indeed sometimes his will must give more regard to his enemy than to his friend. (In saying "bring himself down" I do not mean he would bring himself down from his work completely, for that could not be done without great sin; but from the height of the work, which it is advantageous and necessary to do sometimes, as love demands.)

Nevertheless, in this work he has no leisure to consider who is his friend and who his enemy, who is a relative and who a stranger. I do not say that he will not sometimes, indeed very often, feel a more intimate affection for one, two or three of his friends than he does for all others. This is allowable for many reasons as love demands. For Christ felt a more intimate affection of this kind for John, Mary and Peter than He did for many others.

But I do say that, during this work, all shall be equally dear to him, for he will feel no other ground for affection but only God. So he should love all men plainly and simply for God's sake as well as he loves himself.

For all men were lost in Adam, and all men, that by good works give proof of their will for salvation are saved, or shall be saved, by the Passion of Christ and none other. Not in the same way, but in a similar way, a soul that is perfectly steeped in this work and united to God in spirit (as the experience of this work shows) does all that it can to make all men as proficient in this work as it is itself. For even as when one of our limbs hurts, all the other limbs are in pain and unhealthy on account of it, so if a limb is in good health, all the rest are comfortable as well; and it is the same spiritually with the limbs of the Church. Christ is the head and we are the limbs so long as we are under the rule of love. Whoever would be a perfect disciple of Our Lord must stretch his spirit in this spiritual work for the salvation of all his natural brothers and sisters, as Our Lord did his body on the cross. How?—Not only for his friends, his relatives and those he loved best, but generally, for all mankind without any distinction between one and another. For all that leave sin and ask for mercy shall be saved by virtue of His Passion.

What has been said about humility and charity applies equally to all the other virtues. For they are all subtly comprehended in this little act of love we touched on before.

THE TWENTY-SIXTH CHAPTER

That without much special grace, or common grace over a long period, the work of this book is most laborious; and which part of this work is the work of the soul helped by grace and which is the work of God alone

Therefore labour vigorously for a short while and beat upon the high cloud of unknowing, and rest afterwards. Nonetheless, whoever shall accustom himself to this work will have hard labour. Yes indeed!—Very hard labour, unless he has a more special grace or else has practised it for a long time.

But I pray you, of what does this labour consist? Certainly not in the devout impulse of love that is continually worked in his will, not by himself but by the hand of Almighty God, who is always ready to carry out this work in each soul that is disposed to it, and does all that it can, and has done so for a long time already, to make itself capable of this work.

But I pray you, of what does the labour consist? Most certainly is consists entirely of treading down the memory of all created things that God ever made, and holding them under the cloud of forgetting described earlier. In this does all the labour lie, for it is man's work with the help of grace; while the other, which is mentioned above, that is to say the impulse of love, that is God's work alone. Therefore, do your part of the work, and I make you a sure promise that He will not fail in His.

Act vigorously then; let us see how you stand up to it. Do you not see how He stands and waits for you? Shame on you!—Labour vigorously for a while, and you will soon be relieved of the burden and the hardness of this labour. For though it is hard and strenuous in the beginning when you have no devotion, nevertheless afterwards, when you have devotion, it will be made very restful and very light for you, although before it was so hard, and you will have little labour or none. Then sometimes God will carry on the work by Himself; not all the time, nor for a long period at a stretch, but when He pleases and as He pleases, and then you will think it delightful to leave it to Him.

He will perhaps, at some time, send out a beam of spiritual light that pierces the cloud of unknowing that is between you and Him, and show you some of His secrets which no man can nor may put into words. Then you will feel your affection ablaze with the fire of His love, far more than I can tell you, or may or will at this time. For of that work that belongs only to God I dare not take upon myself to speak with my babbling carnal tongue; and to put it shortly, even if I dared I would not. But of that work that belongs to man, when he feels himself stirred up and helped by grace, I am very glad to tell you: for this is the less perilous of the two.

THE TWENTY-SEVENTH CHAPTER

Who should undertake the work of grace that is described in this book

First and foremost I will tell you who should labour at this work, and when, and by what means; and what discretion you must have in it.

If you ask me who should carry on this work, I reply: "All that have sincerely forsaken the world, and for that reason have not given themselves to active life, but to that life which is contemplative. All these should work in this grace and this work whoever they may be, and whether they are habitual sinners or not".

THE TWENTY-EIGHTH CHAPTER

That no man should presume to undertake this work before his conscience is cleansed of all his besetting sins in accordance with the laws of the Church

If you ask me when they should undertake this work, then I will answer you and say: "Not until after they have cleansed their conscience of all their special deeds of sin which they formerly committed, according to the ordinances of Holy Church."

For by this work, a soul dries up in itself all the ground and root of sin which always remains in it after confession, however earnest it may have been. Therefore, whoever would labour at this work, let him first cleanse his conscience and then, when he has done all that he can according to the laws of the Church, let him set himself boldly and humbly to this work. And let him think that he has been kept from it for too long, for this is a work at which a soul should labour all its lifetime, even though it has never committed mortal sin. While a soul is dwelling in this mortal body it will always see and feel this hampering cloud of unknowing between it and its God. Not only that, but through the bitter consequences of original sin, it will always see and feel some of all those created things that God ever made, or some of their works or actions, continually inserting themselves into his memory between him and his God.

This is a just judgement of God, that man, who when he had sovereignty and lordship over all other created things, nonetheless wilfully made himself subservient to the promptings of his subjects, forsaking the commands of his God and Maker, should afterwards, when he wanted to do God's bidding, see and feel all creatures which should have been beneath him proudly force their way in above him, between him and his God.

THE TWENTY-NINTH CHAPTER

That a man should patiently labour at this work and bear the pain of it and judge no man

Whoever desires to recover the purity he lost through sin, and to win that state of wellbeing where there is no more sorrow at all, must patiently toil at this work and suffer the pain of it, whatever state he is in, whether he has been a habitual sinner or not.

All men have hard labour in this work whether they are sinners or innocent men who never sinned greatly. But those who have been sinners will undergo much greater labour than those who have not, and with good reason. Nevertheless it often happens that some who have been horrible and habitual sinners may reach the perfection of this work sooner than those who have not. This is a miracle of mercy from Our Lord who gives His grace in this way specially, to the wonder of all the world.

Now truly I believe that the Day of Judgement will be glorious, when God shall be seen clearly, and all His gifts. Then some that are now despised and considered of little or no account as common sinners, even perhaps some that are now accounted horrible sinners, will sit, as they deserve, with the Saints, in His presence. While some of those who seem now to be very holy and are reverenced by men as angels, and perhaps some of those who have never yet committed mortal sin shall sit in deep sorrow amid the spawn of Hell.

From this you can see that no man should be judged by another here in this mortal life for the good nor the evil that they do. Indeed the act may be properly assessed, but not the men whether they are good or evil.

THE THIRTIETH CHAPTER

Who should blame and reprove the faults of others?

But I pray you, who should assess men's deeds? Truly those who have authority and care of their souls, either given publicly by the statutes and ordinances of Holy Church, or else privately, in spirit, by a special impulse of the Holy Spirit in perfect love.

Let each man take care that he does not presume to take upon himself the task of blaming and reproving other men's faults, unless he feels truly that he is stirred up by the Holy Spirit within to do this work; or else he may very easily err in his judgements. So beware! Judge yourself if you wish; that is a matter between you and your God, or you and your spiritual director. But leave other men alone.

THE THIRTY-FIRST CHAPTER

How a man should set himself at the beginning of this work against all thoughts and stirrings of sin

From the time when you feel that you have done all that you can to make amends lawfully according to the judgement of Holy Church, set yourself vigorously to carry out this work. Then, if it happens that your memory of any particular past misdeeds, or any new thought or impulse to any other sin will keep pushing into your mind between you and your God, you must resolutely step above it with a fervent impulse of love, and tread it down under your feet and endeavour to cover it with a thick cloud of forgetting, as if it had never been committed in your experience, by you or by any other man. If it often rises, often put it down: in short, put it down as often as it rises.

If you find the labour very great, you may seek tricks, methods and secret refinements of spiritual devices to get rid of it. These devices are better learned from God by experience than from any man alive.

THE THIRTY-SECOND CHAPTER

Of two spiritual devices that may be helpful to the spiritual beginner in this work

Nevertheless I shall tell you something of these devices as I see them. Try them and do better if you can. Do as much as you can to behave as if you did not know that these thoughts were inserting themselves so vigorously between you and your God. Try to look as it were over their shoulders, searching for something else: something that is God, hidden in a cloud of unknowing.

If you do this, I believe that within a short time you will be relieved of your labour. I believe that if this device is well

53

and truly understood, it is nothing else than a longing desire for God, to see Him and feel Him as far as you can in this life. Such a desire is charity, and deserves always to give easement.

Another device is this;—try it if you wish. When you feel that you can in no way put these thoughts down, cringe down before them like a cowardly captive conquered in battle. Think that it is but folly for you to strive against them any longer, and therefore yield yourself up to God while in the hands of your enemies, and feel in yourself that you are overthrown for ever.

Take good heed of this device I beg you, for I think that in applying it you should be melted all to water. Certainly I think if this device is truly understood it is nothing else than a true knowledge and feeling of yourself as you are, a wretch, a piece of dirt, far worse than nothing. This knowledge and feeling is humility: and this humility deserves to have God Himself descending in His might to avenge you on your enemies; and to take you up and fondly dry your spiritual eyes, as a father does his child that was on the point of perishing in the jaws of savage swine or baleful biting bears.

THE THIRTY-THIRD CHAPTER

How in this work the soul is cleansed both from its besetting sins and from the pain of them, and how there is no perfect rest in this life

I will not tell you about any more devices at this time. For if you have grace to put these to the test, I believe that you will be better able to teach me than I you.

For although it should be as I say, I think that I am very far from attaining it myself. Therefore I pray you that you help me and act both for yourself and for me.

Go on then, labour vigorously for a time I pray you, and

humbly suffer the pain even if you cannot easily implement these devices. For truly this is your Purgatory. When the pain has passed away, and when your devices are given by God and through grace have become a habit; then I do not doubt that you will be cleansed, not only from sin but from the pain it brings. I mean the pain of your former besetting sins, not the pain of original sin. For that pain will always remain with you whatever you do until the day of your death. Nevertheless, it will do you little harm in comparison with the pain arising form your besetting sins; and yet you will not be without great labour. For out of this original sin will always spring up new and fresh impulses of sin, which you must always strike down and be diligent to cut away with the sharp sword of discretion. From this you can see and learn that there is no security nor any real rest in this life.

But you must not turn back because of this, nor be too much afraid of failing. For if you may find grace to destroy the pain from your former besetting sins in the manner I have said (or in a better way if you can find a better) then you can be certain that the pain of original sin, or the new impulses of sin that are to come, will be able to do you but little harm.

THE THIRTY-FOURTH CHAPTER

That God gives His grace directly and it cannot be reached except directly

If you ask me by what means you can come to this work, I beseech Almighty God, of His great grace and His great courtesy to teach you Himself. For truly, I do you a good turn in letting you know that I cannot tell you. And no wonder, for this is the work of God alone, specially carried out in that soul that pleases Him without any merit on the part of the soul. For without having this grace, not even a saint or an angel can think of wishing for it.

I believe that Our Lord will grant the carrying out of this work as specially and as often—no! More specially and more often to those who have been habitual sinners than to some who never grieved Him greatly in comparison with them. This He does so that He may be seen to be all-merciful and almighty, and that He may be seen to work as He wishes, where He wishes and when He wishes.

But He does not give this grace nor carry out this work in any soul that is not capable of it; and yet no soul that does not have the grace is capable of having it,—none, whether it is a sinning soul or an innocent one. For it is neither given for innocence nor witheld on account of sin. Take good note that I say "withheld" and not "withdrawn". Beware of error here, I beg you; for always, the nearer men come to reaching the truth, the more careful they must be and wary of error. My meaning is good. If you cannot understand it, leave it on one side until God comes and teaches you. Do this, and you will take no harm.

Beware of pride, for it blasphemes God and His gifts, and makes sinners bold. If you were very humble, you would feel about this work as I say, that God gives it freely and not for merit. The nature of the work is such that its presence enables the soul to have it and feel it and no soul may have that capability without it. The capability is inseparably united with the work itself, so that anyone who has a feeling for this work is able to do it, and no-one else; so much so that without this work a soul is as it were dead, and cannot covet or desire it. To whatever degree you will and desire it, to the same degree you will have it, no more and no less. Yet it is not will nor desire but something else about which you know nothing that stirs you to will and desire the very thing about which you know nothing. Do not worry because you know no more of it I pray you; but work on more and more, so that you are working at it all the time.

To put it shortly, let that thing have its way with you and lead you where it wishes. Let it do the work and you be the patient. Just look at it and leave it alone. Do not interfere with it in an attempt to help it, for fear that you should spoil everything. You be the wood and let it be the carpenter. You be the house and let it be the householder living in it. Be blind for the time, and shear away all desire for knowledge, for it will hinder you more than help you.

It is quite sufficient for you that you feel yourself pleasantly stirred up by something,—you know not what except that in this impulse you have no thought of anything less than God, and your will is directed simply towards God.

If this is so, then have a firm trust that it is God alone who stirs up your will and your desire wholly by Himself and without any means either on His part or on yours. And do not fear the devil, for he may not come so near. He may never come to stir up a man's will except very occasionally and by devices from afar, however subtle a devil he may be. For not even a good angel can stir up your will sufficiently and without means. In short, nothing can but God.

From these words you can understand to some extent, but much more clearly from experience, that in this work man can use no means and that a man cannot come to it through means. All good means depend upon it and it upon no means; nor may any means lead you to it.

THE THIRTY-FIFTH CHAPTER

Of the three ways in which one learning contemplation should be occupied—reading, thinking and praying

Nevertheless there are means with which one learning contemplation should be occupied; they are study, meditation and orison,— or else, so that you may understand them, they may be called reading, thinking and praying.

You will find these three far better written about than I

can teach you in another book[1] by someone else, so there is no need for me to go into the characteristics of them here. I shall only say that these three are so woven together that for beginners and proficients—but not for those who are perfect, in so far as it is possible to be in this life—thinking cannot satisfactorily be attained without reading and hearing coming first. Reading and hearing are really the same. Clerics read books and ignorant men read clerics when they hear them preach the word of God. Beginners and proficients cannot pray properly without thinking coming first. See the proof of this in the same book.

The word of God, whether written or spoken, is like a mirror. Spiritually, the eye of the soul is reason. The conscience is the spiritual face. Just as you understand that if there is a dirty spot on your bodily face, your bodily eye cannot see the spot nor know where it is without a mirror or help from somebody else, so it is in the spiritual sense: without reading or hearing God's word, as far as human understanding goes it is impossible for a soul that is blinded by the habit of sin to see the dirty spot on its conscience. It follows that when a man sees in a physical or spiritual mirror or learns from another man the whereabouts of the dirty spot on his face, either physical or spiritual, then at once, but not before that, he runs to the well to wash. If the spot is besetting sin, then the well is Holy Church, the water Confession and all that goes with it. If it is but a blind root and an impulse of sin, then the well is merciful God, and the water prayer and all that goes with it.

So you can see that beginners and proficients cannot properly come to thinking without reading or hearing coming first, nor to prayer without thinking.

[1] The book referred to may be Guigo II *Scala Claustralium*.

THE THIRTY-SIXTH CHAPTER

Of the meditations of those who continually labour at the work of this book

This is not the case with those who continually labour at the work of this book. Their meditations are, as it were, sudden apprehensions and blind feelings of their own wretchedness and the goodness of God, without any necessity of reading or hearing coming first, and without any special regard for anything less than God. These sudden apprehensions and blind feelings are more quickly learned from God than from man.

I should not care if, at this time, you had no other meditations about your own wretchedness or the goodness of God (I mean if you feel moved to this by grace and counsel) but such as you may have in the word 'sin' or the word 'God' or any other such word as you like, not analysing these words, or expounding them with imaginative ingenuity or examining the nuances of these words as if you would, by this knowledge, increase your devotion. I believe this should never happen in these circumstances and in this work. But keep all these words intact, and mean by 'sin' a lump of you do not know what, but in fact nothing else but yourself. I believe in this sightless vision of sin conceived of as a lump that is nothing else but you yourself, it would be impossible to find a thing more distracted than you would be at that time; and yet perhaps anyone who looked at you would think you soberly disposed, without any change of expression,—sitting, walking, lying, leaning, standing or kneeling in a state of very sane restfulness.

THE THIRTY-SEVENTH CHAPTER

Of the special prayers of those who are continually engaged in the work of this book

Even as the meditations of those who continually engage in this grace and this work rise suddenly, without any means, the same thing happens in their prayers. I mean in their private prayers, not those prayers that are ordained by Holy Church. For true workers in this work reverence no prayer so much as those; and therefore they practise them in the form and according to the rules ordained by the holy fathers before us. But their private prayers rise ever more suddenly to God without any means or special preparation coming first, or going with them. If they are in words, as they seldom are, then they are in very few words, and the fewer the better. Yes, and if it is only a little word of one syllable, I think it is better than two, and more in accordance with the work of the spirit; for the spiritual worker in this work should always be at the highest and the supreme point of the spirit. That this is the truth, we can see by an example from ordinary life. A man or woman frightened by a sudden outbreak of fire, a man's death, or anything else of that kind, suddenly at the height of his spirit is driven in haste and of necessity to cry out or pray for help. How does he do this? Certainly not in many words or a word of two syllables. Why is that? Because he thinks it will take too long to declare the need and the working of his spirit, so he bursts up with a great shout from the depth of his spirit, and cries only one little word of one syllable such as the word "fire" or the word "help".

And just as this little word "fire" stirs the hearers more powerfully and pierces their ears more quickly, so with a little word of one syllable when it is not only spoken or thought, but secretly meant in the depth of the spirit,— which is also the height, for in spiritual things all are one, height and depth, length and breadth—it pierces the ears of Almighty God more than does any long psalm unmindfully mumbled through the teeth. Therefore it is written: "A short prayer pierces heaven".

THE THIRTY-EIGHTH CHAPTER
How and why a short prayer penetrates Heaven

Why does this little short prayer of one little syllable penetrate heaven? Certainly because it is prayed with a full spirit in the height, the depth, the length and the breadth of his spirit who prayed it. It is in the height because it is with all the might of the spirit. It is in the depth because in this little syllable is contained all the wisdom of the spirit. It is in the length because if it could always feel as it feels, it would always cry out as it cries. It is in the breadth because it wishes for all others what it wishes for itself. It is at this time that a soul comprehended, after the teaching of St. Paul[1] with all the saints—(not fully, but in the manner and degree which accords with this work)—the length, breadth, height and depth of eternal, all-loving, almighty, all-wise God. The eternity of God is His length. His love is His breadth. His might is His height. His wisdom is His depth. No wonder, then, if a soul which is so nearly conformed by grace to the image and likeness of God its Maker is soon heard by God. Yes, even if it is a very sinful soul which is as it were an enemy of God; if it might by grace manage to cry out such a little syllable from the height, depth, length and breadth of its spirit, then it would, because of the anguished sound of that cry, always be heard and helped by God.

Let us take an example. If you should hear him who is your deadly enemy cry out from fear in the height of his spirit the little word "fire!" or the word "help!"; then with-

[1] Eph. III. 18.

out any consideration that he is your enemy, but from pure pity in your heart stirred up and raised by the anguish of his cry, you would get up, although it was a night in midwinter, and help him to put out the fire, or soothe and comfort him in his distress.

O Lord! Since a man may be made so merciful through grace and have so much mercy and pity for his enemy in spite of his enmity; what pity and mercy shall God have for a spiritual cry in the soul, made and fashioned in the height, depth, length and breadth of his spirit,–seeing that God has everything by nature that man has by grace, and much more? Certainly He will have much more mercy beyond comparison, since it is a fact that what is had by nature is much nearer to each thing than what is had by grace.

THE THIRTY-NINTH CHAPTER

How the perfect worker should pray. What prayer is in itself, and if a man prays in words, what words are best suited to the special quality of prayer

Therefore we must pray in the height and depth, length and breadth of our spirit, and that not in many words, but in a little word of one syllable. What shall this word be? Certainly such a word is best suited to the special quality of prayer. And what word is that? Let us first see what prayer really is in itself, and after that we can know more clearly what word is best suited to the special quality of prayer.

Prayer in itself is really nothing else than a devout intent directed towards God for getting what is good and removing what is evil. So, since it is a fact that all evils are comprehended in the word "sin", either by cause or by being, let us therefore, when we earnestly pray for the removal of evil, neither say nor think, nor mean anything else, nor use more words than the little word "sin". And if we earnestly pray for getting what is good, let us cry, either in word or in thought or in desire, nothing else and no more words than the word "God". For in God are all good things, both by cause and by being.

You should not be surprised that I choose these words before all others. If I knew any shorter words so fully comprehending in themselves all good and all evil as these two words, or if I had been taught by God to take any other words, I would have taken them and discarded these; and I counsel you to do the same.

Do not study any words, for by doing so you will never come to your purpose nor to this work, for it can never be got by study, only by grace. Therefore take no other words for your prayer—although I set out these here—than such as God moves you to use. Nevertheless, if God moves you to use these, I counsel you not to leave them,—I mean, if you are going to pray in words, and not otherwise,—because they are very short words.

Although the shortness of the prayer is greatly recommended here, there is no restraint at all on the frequency of the prayer. For as was said before, it is prayed in the length of the spirit so that it should never cease until everything it longs for has been fully obtained. We have an example of this in the man or woman frightened in the way we spoke about before. For we see that they never stop crying out this little word "help" or this little word "fire" until they have got a great deal of help in their trouble.

THE FORTIETH CHAPTER

While engaged in this work a soul has no special regard to any one vice in itself nor to any one virtue in itself

In the same manner you must fill your spirit with the spiritual meaning of the word "sin", without any special regard to the kind of sin, whether it is venial or mortal: pride, wrath, envy, covetousness, sloth, gluttony or lust. What concern is it to contemplatives what the sin is or how great the sin is? During this work they think each sin is great in itself, since the least sin draws them away from God and deprives them of their spiritual peace.

Feel sin a lump, you know not of what; in fact, nothing else but yourself. Cry out spiritually always the same cry: "Sin! Sin! Sin!—Help! Help! Help!" This spiritual cry is better learned from God by experience than from any man's teaching. For it is best when it is purely in spirit without any special thought or any pronouncing of the word; except on very rare occasions, when from the fullness of the spirit it breaks out into words, since soul and body are both filled with the sorrow and the burden of sin.

You must act in the same way with the little word "God". Fill your spirit with the spiritual meaning of it, without any special regard to any of His works, whether they are good, better or best of all, physically or spiritually; or to any virtue that may be performed by grace, whether it is humility, charity, patience, abstinence, faith, hope, sobriety, chastity or voluntary poverty.

What concern is this to contemplatives? For all virtues they find and feel in God; for in Him is everything, both by cause and by being. They think that if they had God, they would have all that is good; therefore they covet nothing especially but only good God. You must act in the same manner as far as you can by grace, and mean God wholly, and wholly God, so that nothing works in your mind and in your will but only God.

And because all the while you live this wretched life you must always feel to some extent that foul, stinking lump of sin, as it were united and congealed with the substance of your being: therefore you shall mean these two words alternately: sin and God, with the general understanding that if you had God you would lack sin, and that if you might lack sin, you should have God.

THE FORTY-FIRST CHAPTER

In any other work less important than this, men should have discretion, but in this, none

Furthermore, if you ask me what discretion you shall have in this work, then I give you the answer: "None at all". For in all other acts you shall have discretion, as in eating, drinking and sleeping, in keeping your body from excessive cold and heat, in long prayer and reading, and in carrying on conversation with your fellow Christians. In all these you shall have discretion so that they are neither too much nor too little; but in this work you shall keep to no measure, for I wish you should never cease form this work as long as you live.

I do not say that you will always be able to continue in this work as fresh as ever. This is not possible. For sometimes sickness or other distempers in body and soul, as well as other necessities of nature, will greatly hinder you and draw you down from the perfection of this work. But I do say that you must always have it, either in earnest or in play, that is to say either actually working at it or having it in your will to do so.

Therefore for God's love take care of your health as far as you can, so that as much as it lies in your power you may not be yourself responsible for your bodily weakness; for I truly tell you that this work requires a great serenity and a very whole and clean disposition both in body and soul.

Therefore for the love of God act sensibly both in body and soul, so as to keep in good health as far as you can. But if sickness comes in spite of your precautions, have patience and wait humbly for God's mercy: and all is good enough. For I tell you truly that patience in sickness and other troubles of all kinds pleases God much more than any pleasurable devotion you may show when you are well.

THE FORTY-SECOND CHAPTER

*By acting without discretion in this, men will remain
discreet in everything else; otherwise they never will*

Perhaps you are going to ask me how you should exercise
discretion in eating, in sleeping and in all other things. I can
answer this question very shortly: "Accept what comes
your way". Carry on this work without stopping and without discretion and you will easily know when to begin and
when to stop in all your other actions with a great deal of
discretion. For I cannot believe that a soul continuing in this
work night and day without discretion would go astray.

Therefore, if I could give an alert and careful attention to
this spiritual work within my soul, I would have a heedlessness in eating, drinking, sleeping, speaking, or any other
outward action. For I truly believe that I should come to
discretion in these things rather by such a heedlessness than
by attending to them carefully in order to set targets and
limits. In fact I could never achieve it by such means in spite
of everything I could do or say.

Let men say what they will and let experience judge.
Therefore lift up your heart with a blind stirring of love, and
mean now sin, now God. You wish to have God, you wish
to lack sin; God you are lacking, sin you have securely. Now
may good God help you, for now you have need.

THE FORTY-THIRD CHAPTER

*That the knowledge and awareness of a man's own being
must of necessity be lost if the perfection of the work is to
be truly felt by any soul in this life*

See that nothing works in your mind or your will except
God alone. Try to put a stop to all knowledge and feeling of
anything less than God, and tread it down very far under the
cloud of forgetting. You must understand that in this work

you must not only forget all other created things than yourself, and their actions and yours, but also in this work you must forget both yourself and the deeds you have done in God's service, as well as all other created things and their actions.

For this is the condition of the perfect lover, that not only does he love the thing that he loves more than himself, but also, in a way, he hates himself for the sake of the thing that he loves. You must deal with yourself like this: you must hate and grow weary of everything that works in your mind and in your will except God alone. For otherwise the thing, whatever it is, is between you and your God. No wonder then that you loathe and hate to think about yourself, when you always feel sin a foul stinking lump, you do not know of what, between you and your God,— and this lump is nothing else but yourself. For you must realise that it is united and congealed with the substance of your being as it were without separation.

Therefore, do away with all thoughts and feelings of all creatures, but most diligently of yourself. For on the awareness and feeling of yourself depends awareness and feeling of all other creatures; and compared with this, all other creatures are easily forgotten. For if you will diligently make trial of this, you will find that when you have forgotten all other creatures and all their actions—and your own actions as well—there will remain, even after that, a simple awareness and feeling of your own being between you and your God; and this awareness and feeling must always be destroyed before you can truly experience the perfection of this work.

THE FORTY-FOURTH CHAPTER

*How a soul must dispose itself so as to destroy all
knowledge and awareness of its own being*

Now you ask me how you may destroy this bare awareness
and feeling of your own being. For perhaps you think that if
it were destroyed all other hindrances would be destroyed. If
you think this, your think very truly. But I say in reply, that
without a full measure of special grace given quite freely by
God, and in addition a corresponding capacity to receive the
grace on your part, this bare awareness and feeling of your
own being can in no way be destroyed.

This capacity is nothing else than a strong and deep spiritual sorrow. But in this sorrow you must exercise discretion in the following manner; you must, in the time of
sorrow, take care that you do not put too great a strain on
your body or your spirit. Sit quite still as if simulating sleep,
worn out and drowned in sorrow. This is true sorrow, this is
perfect sorrow, and well it is for him who can win to this
sorrow.

All men have grounds for sorrow, but most of all he
whose grounds for sorrow are that he knows and feels that
he is. All other sorrows in comparison with this are as it
were make-belief to reality. He may feel sorrow deeply
who knows and feels not only what he is but that he is. He
who has not felt this sorrow, let him be sorrowful because he
has not yet felt perfect sorrow. This sorrow, when a man has
it, cleanses the soul not only of sin but also of the punishment it has deserved for sin; and moreover it makes a soul
more able to receive that joy which snatches away from a
man all awareness and feeling of his own being.

This sorrow, if it is truly understood, is full of holy desire;
otherwise a man in this life could not endure or bear it. Were
it not that a soul were to some extent nourished with a sort of
comfort from the proper performance of its work, it would

not be able to bear the pain that it has from the awareness and feeling of its own being.

For as often as a man would have a true awareness and feeling of his God in purity of spirit as far as is possible in this life, he finds that he is not able to. For he always finds his awareness and feeling as it were occupied and filled with a foul stinking lump of himself, which must always be hated, despised and forsaken if he would be God's perfect disciple as taught by God Himself in the mount of perfection. Whenever this happens he goes almost mad with sorrow, so that he weeps and wails, struggles, curses and swears; and to be brief, he thinks the burden of himself which he bears so heavy that he does not care what becomes of him, so long as God is pleased. Yet in all this sorrow, he has no desire to end his existence, for that would be the devil's madness and an insult to God. But he is very glad to be alive, and offers very hearty thanks to God for the great worth and gift of his existence, although he constantly desires to lose the awareness and feeling of his existence.

This sorrow and desire each soul must have and feel in itself, either in this or in some other way; as God grants in teaching His spiritual disciples according to His good pleasure and their corresponding capacity in body, in soul, in degree and in disposition, before the time that they are perfectly united with God in perfect love,—as far as may be experienced in this life,—if God grants it.

THE FORTY-FIFTH CHAPTER

A clear statement of certain deceptions which may occur in this work

I tell you this, that in this work a young disciple who has not been thoroughly practised and tried in spiritual working may easily be deceived; and unless he soon takes warning and has the grace to leave off and submit himself to spiritual direction, he may perhaps have his bodily powers destroyed, and his spiritual faculties fall into fantasy. All this is due to pride, sensuality and intellectual speculation.

The deception may come about like this. A young man or a woman newly attached to the school of devotion hears this sorrow and this desire read or spoken about; and how a man should lift up his heart to God and unceasingly desire to feel the love of his God. At once in their foolish speculation they understand the words not spiritually, as they were intended, but physically and materially, and work their fleshly hearts outrageously in their breasts. So through lack of grace, as they deserve, and their own pride and speculation, they strain their veins and their bodily powers so inhumanly and roughly that, within a short time they either fall into frenzies, weariness and a kind of listless feebleness of body and soul, which makes them go out of themselves and seek some vain fleshly and bodily comfort outside, as it were, for the recreation of body and soul[1]; or if they do not fall into this, they deserve on account of their spiritual blindness, and of the fleshly irritation of their nature in their bodily breasts at the time of their pretended animal not spiritual working, to have their breasts inflamed with an unnatural heat caused by misuse of their bodies in this pretended work; or else they conceive a false heat engendered by the devil, their spiritual enemy, caused by their pride, sensuality and speculative mind. And yet perhaps they think that it is the fire of love given and kindled by the grace and goodness of the Holy Spirit. Truly, from this deceit and its offshoots spring many evils: much hypocrisy, much heresy and much error. For soon after such false feelings comes a false knowledge learned in the devil's school, just as after a true feeling comes a true knowledge learned in God's school. For I tell you truly, the devil has his contemplatives just as God has His.

This deceit of false feeling and false knowledge following

---

[1] An attack on the teaching of Richard Rolle.

on it has diverse and extraordinary variations owing to the diverse states and subtle differences of disposition of those who are deceived; as also have the true feelings and knowledge of those who are saved.

But I will not detail any more deceptions here than those with which I think you may be assailed if ever you propose to take up this work. For what profit would it be to you to know how these great scholars and men and women of other degree than yours are deceived? Indeed, none at all.

Therefore I am telling you no more than those which are likely to happen to you if you labour at this work: I tell you this much, that you may beware of them in your work if you should be assailed by them.

THE FORTY-SIXTH CHAPTER

Some sound teaching how a man may escape these deceptions, and work more with eagerness of spirit than with any rough bodily strength

Therefore for God's love take care in this work, and do not strain the heart in your breast over-roughly or beyond measure; but work rather with eagerness than with any brute force. For the more eagerly you work, the more humbly and spiritually; but the more roughly, the more bodily and bestially.

Therefore, take care,[1] for certainly any bestial heart that presumes to touch the high mountain of this work will be driven away with stones. Stones are hard and dry by nature, and cause great pain where they hit; and certainly such rough strainings are very hard fastened in the fleshliness of bodily feeling, and very dry, lacking the dew of grace,—they hurt the silly soul grievously and make it fester in fantasy feigned by fiends. Therefore beware of this brutal roughness, and

[1] Hebrews XII. 20 from Exodus XIX. 13.

learn to love eagerly, with a mild and gentle demeanour as well in body as in soul; wait courteously and humbly the will of Our Lord, and do not snatch over-hastily like a greedy greyhound, however hungry you may be. And—to speak lightly—I adivse you as far as you can to refrain from rough and great stirrings of your spirit, just as if you would in no way let Him know how desirous you are to have Him and see Him and feel Him.

Perhaps you think that this is childishly and playfully spoken. But I believe that whoever has the grace to do and feel as I say would find himself having good playful fun with Him as a father does with a child, kissing him and embracing him, and happy he should be.

THE FORTY-SEVENTH CHAPTER

A wise instruction on the purity of spirit demanded in this work, declaring how a soul should show his desire to God in one way, and in quite a different way to man

Do not be surprised that I speak thus childishly and, as it were, foolishly, and without natural discretion. I do it for certain reasons, and I think I have been stirred up for many days to feel like this, think like this and speak like this, to other of my special friends in God as well as to you now. One of the reasons why I bid you hide from God the desire of your heart is this: I hope that by this hiding it should come more clearly to His knowledge, to your profit and the fulfilling of your desire, than it would by any other method of showing that I believe you would be able to master.

Another reason is that I would by such a concealed showing bring you out of the crude state of bodily feeling into the purity and depth of spiritual feeling; and furthermore to help you at last to tie the spiritual knot of burning love between you and your God in spiritual unity and accordance of will.

You know well that God is a spirit; and whoever would be

united with Him, it must be in truthfulness and depth of spirit, very far from any counterfeit bodily thing. Truly all things are known to God and nothing can be hidden from His knowledge, either bodily or spiritual.

But since God is a spirit, that which is hidden in the depths of the spirit is more clearly known and shown to Him than that which is mingled with anything bodily. Any bodily thing is, in the course of nature, further from God than anything spiritual. From this reasoning it seems that while our desire is mingled with anything bodily, as it is when we strive and strain ourselves body and soul together, it is so much the further from God than it would be if it were done more devoutly and more eagerly in soberness and purity and in the depths of the spirit.

Here you may see, at least in part, why I bid you so childishly to conceal and hide the impulse of your desire for God. Yet I do not tell you simply to hide it; for that were the bidding of a fool, to tell you simply to do that which cannot in any way be done. But I tell you to do all that you can to hide it. I tell you this because truly I would have you cast it into the depths of your spirit, far from any crude mingling with anything bodily, which would make it less spiritual and therefore that much further from God.

For I know well that the more your soul has of spirituality the less it has of the bodily; the nearer it is to God, the better it pleases Him, and the more clearly it may be seen by Him. Not that His sight may at any time or in anything be more clear than in another, for it is unchangeable: but it is more like Him when it is in purity of spirit, for He is a spirit.

There is another reason why I bid you do what you can not to let Him know. You and I and many others like us, are so liable to understand a thing physically which is meant spiritually that perhaps, if I had advised you to show to God the impulse of your heart, you would have made a physical showing to Him, either by expression or voice or word, or by some other rough bodily straining, as happens when you

73

are showing what is hidden in your heart to another man; and to that degree your work would have been impure. For in one way a thing should be shown to man, and in quite another way to God.

THE FORTY-EIGHTH CHAPTER

How God would be served both with body and soul and rewards men in both, and how men may know when all those sounds and delights that fall upon the body during prayer are good, and when evil

I do not say this because I want you to desist if at any time you feel stirred to pray in words, or from the abundance of devotion in your spirit to burst out and speak to God as to a man, and say some good words as you feel impelled, such as: "Good Jesus", "Fair Jesus", "Sweet Jesus" and other such words. No! God forbid that you should take it so! For indeed I do not mean that at all,—God forbid that I should separate what God has joined together, body and spirit. For God would be served with body and soul together as is proper and gives man his heavenly reward, both in body and soul.

As a foretaste of that reward He will sometimes set aflame the body of one of His devout servants here in this life with wonderful delights and comforts, not once or twice, but perhaps very often and as He pleases. Of these, some do not come from without into the body through the windows of the senses, but from within, rising and springing up from the abundance of spiritual gladness and true devotion in the spirit. Such comforts and such delights are not to be held suspect; and to be brief, I believe that anyone who has experienced them could not hold them suspect.

But all other comforts, sounds, gladness and delights that come from without suddenly and you do not know where they are from, I beg you hold them suspect. For they can be both good and evil, brought about by a good angel if they are good, or a bad angel if they are evil. But they can in no way be evil if the deceits of speculative thought and uncontrolled straining of the fleshy heart are removed as I teach you, or by some better means if you can find a better.

Why is this? Certainly on account of the cause of this comfort, that is to say the devout impulse of love which exists in the pure spirit. This is formed by the hand of God without any means; therefore it must be far removed from any fantasy or false opinion that may come to a man in this life.

As to other comforts, sounds and delights, and how you should tell whether they are good or evil, I do not intend to tell you about them at this time, because I think there is no need. You can find it written in another place in another man's book[1] a thousand times better than I can write or say it; as also you may find this that I have set out here, far better than it is here. But what does it matter? I shall not cease on that account, nor will it give me trouble to fulfil the desire and impulse of your heart towards me; which you have shown me that you have, by your words of old and now by your actions.

But I will say this to you about the sounds and delights which come in by the windows of the senses and can be both good and evil. Continually use this blind, devout and eager impulse of love that I am telling you about: and then I have no doubt that it will give you good knowledge of them, even if it is rather astonished by them the first time, because they are strange. Yet it will do this for you. It will bind your heart so fast that you will not in any way give much credence to them until they are verified for you, either from within wonderfully by the Spirit of God, or else from without by the counsel of some discreet director.

---

[1] One 15th-Century manuscript has the note, "Hiltons".

THE FORTY-NINTH CHAPTER

*That the substance of all perfection lies in nothing else but
a good will; and how all sounds, comforts and delights
that may happen in this life are in comparison nothing but
as it were accidents*

Therefore I pray you, incline eagerly to this humble impulse
of love in your heart, and follow after it; for it will be your
guide in this life, and bring you to heaven in the next. It is the
substance of all good living, and without it no good work
can be begun nor ended, for it is nothing else than a good
will in conformity with God, and a sort of satisfaction and
gladness that you feel in your will for all that He does.

Such a good will is the substance of all perfection. All
delights and comforts, bodily and spiritual, in comparison
with this are as it were accidents, however holy they may be;
and they do but depend on this goodwill. I call them accidents, because you can either have them or lack them without any damage. I mean in this life, but it is not so in the bliss
of heaven; for there they will be united with the substance
without separation, even as the body in which they are
working will be with the soul; so that the substance of them
here is but a good spiritual will.

I truly believe that for him who feels the perfection of this
will, as far as he can here, there is no delight or comfort that
can come in this life that he is not as willing and glad to lack
as to have and to feel, if such is God's will.

THE FIFTIETH CHAPTER

*What chaste love is; and how in some creatures such
sensual comforts seldom occur, in others very often*

Hereby you may see that we should direct all our attention
to this meek impulse of love in our will; and to all other
delights and comforts bodily and spiritual, however pleas-

ant and holy they may be, (if it is courteous and proper to say so), we should have a sort of indifference. If they come, welcome them, but do not rely too much on them for fear they enfeeble you: for it will take a very great deal of your strength to remain for any long time in such sweet feelings and tears.

It may be, too, that you will be stirred to love God for their sake: you will know that this is so if you grumble too much when they are taken away. If such is the case then your love is not yet chaste nor perfect. For love which is chaste and perfect, although it allows the body to be fed and comforted by the presence of such feelings and tears, none-theless it does not grumble but is well satisfied when they are lacking, since it is God's will. Yet in some people this love is not ordinarily without such comforts, and in other people such delights and comforts occur but seldom.

All this is according to the disposition and ordinance of God, and all for the profit and needs of different people. For some people are so weak and tender in spirit that if they were not somewhat comforted by feeling such delights, they might in no way endure nor bear the diversity of temp-tations and tribulations that they suffer and are burdened with in this life at the hands of their bodily and spiritual enemies.

And there are some who are so weak in body that they are not able to undertake any great penance to cleanse them of their sins: these people Our Lord will very graciously cleanse in spirit by such delightful feelings and tears.

Also, on the other hand, there are some people so strong in spirit that they can gather comfort enough within their souls by offering up this reverent and humble impulse of love and accordance of will; so they do not need much to be fed with such sweet comforts in their bodily feelings. Which of these is holier and dearer to God? God knows, not I.

THE FIFTY-FIRST CHAPTER

*That men should take great care that they do not
understand in a bodily sense what is meant in a spiritual
sense; and especially, it is a good thing to be very careful
in understanding the words "in" and "up"*

Therefore incline humbly to this blind impulse of love in
your heart. I do not mean in your bodily heart, but in your
spiritual heart which is your will. Be very careful that you do
not understand materially that which is spoken spiritually.
For I can tell you truly that the bodily and material concepts
of those who have speculative and imaginative minds are the
cause of much error. You may see an example of this when I
tell you to hide your desire for God as much as you can. For
perhaps if I had told you to show your desire to God you
would have understood it in a more bodily sense than you do
now when I bid you hide it. For you know well that everything that is deliberately hidden is cast into the depths of the
spirit. So I think there is great need to have much caution in
understanding words that are spoken in a spiritual sense, so
that you conceive them not bodily but spiritually as they
were meant. And especially it is wise to be careful with the
word "in" and the word "up". For I think in the misunderstanding of these two words lies much error and much
deception in those who intend to be spiritual workers. Some
of this I have learned by experience, some by hearsay, and I
want to tell you a little of my thoughts on these deceptions.

A young disciple in God's school, newly turned away
from the world considers that through the little time he has
given in confession, he is able to take upon himself spiritual
work about which he hears those around him speak or read,
or perhaps reads himself. Therefore when such people read
or hear talk of spiritual work, especially the following:—
"how a man shall draw all his mental powers within himself", or "how he shall climb above himself", at once,

78

through blindness of soul, fleshliness and natural curiosity of mind, they misunderstand these words, and, because they find in themselves a natural desire for hidden things, they consider that they are called to this work by grace. Indeed, if their director does not agree that they should work at this work, soon they feel a sort of resentment against the director, and think, (yes indeed, and perhaps say to others who are like them),—that they cannot find anybody who can really understand what they mean and therefore at once, owing to the boldness and presumptuous curiosity of their minds, they leave off humble prayer and penance too soon and set themselves, as they think, to a most spiritual work within their souls.

This work, if it is properly understood, is neither bodily nor spiritual work and, to be brief, it is work against nature and the devil is the chief worker of it. It is the easiest way to death of the body and the soul, for it is madness and not wisdom, and leads a man on to madness. Yet they do not think so; for they intend in this work to think of nothing but God.

THE FIFTY-SECOND CHAPTER

How young, presumptuous disciples misunderstand the word "in"; and the errors that result from it

The madness of which I speak occurs like this. They read or hear it well said that they should leave the outward working of their minds and work inwards; and because they do not know what inward working is, they work in the wrong way. For they turn the bodily senses inwards to their bodies against the course of nature, and strain them as though they would see inwards with their bodily eyes, hear inwards with their ears, and so on with all their senses—smell, taste and feeling turned inwards.

Thus they reverse the course of nature, and with this

curiosity they labour their imagination so indiscreetly that at last they turn the brain in their heads. Then at once the devil has power to fabricate some false light or sounds, sweet scents in their noses, wonderful tastes in their mouths; and many strange heats and burnings in their bodily breasts, in their backs, or in their kidneys or in their loins.

Yet in this fantasy they think that they have a restful contemplation of their God without any hindrance of vain thoughts; and certainly they have it in a manner, for they are so filled with falshood that vanity does not affect them. Why is this? Because the same fiend that should administer vain thoughts to them if they were in a good way, the same is the chief instigator of this work; and you must well understand that he would not hinder himself, and he does not take from them the remembrance of God for fear that he should be suspected.

THE FIFTY-THIRD CHAPTER

Of various inadequate practices that result from a man not following the work of this book

Many extraordinary habits are found amongst those that are led astray into this false work and its varieties, far more than are found in those who are God's true disciples, who always behave seemly in all their practices, bodily and spiritual. But it is not so with these others. If anyone should see them as they sit at this time, if their eyes were open, he would see them glaring as if they were mad, and moreover, looking as if they saw the devil. And certainly it is good that they should be wary, for truly the fiend is not far off. Some have a fixed stare as if they were sheep affected by brain disease, stricken in the head and likely soon to die. Some hang their heads on one side as if there were a worm in their ear. Some speak in a piping voice as if there were no spirit in their bodies; and this is the proper condition of a hypocrite. Some cry and whine in their throats, so greedy and hasty are they to say what they think; and this is the condition of heretics, and of those who with presumption and curiosity of mind will always maintain error.

Many disordered and strange practices follow on this error, if anyone could see them all. Some of these men, indeed, are so clever that they can refrain from such acts for the most part when they are in company. But if you saw them in places where they were at home, then I think these things would not be hidden. And further, I believe that if anyone should bluntly gainsay their opinion he would soon see them burst out in some way. And yet they think that all they ever do is for the love of God and to maintain the truth. Now indeed, I believe that unless God shows His miraculous mercy to make them leave off soon, they will love God so long in this manner that they will go staring mad to the devil. I do not say that the devil has such a perfect servant in this life, that he is deceived and infected by all the fantasies I set out here,—and yet it may be there is one or many a one who is infected with them all. But I do say that he has no perfect hypocrite or heretic on earth that is not guilty of some of the things I have said, or perhaps shall say if God permits.

Some men are so burdened with strange practices in their behaviour that when they hear anything, they twist their heads quaintly to one side, and up with their chins; they gape with their mouths as if they would hear with them and not with their ears. Some, when they come to speak, jab with their fingers either their other hand, or their own breast or the breast of those they are talking to. Some can neither stand still or sit still nor lie still unless they are wagging their feet or else doing something with their hands. Some row with their arms in time with their speaking, as if they had to swim over a great stretch of water. Some are continually smiling and laughing at every other word they say, as if they were giggling girls or silly japing jugglers misbehaving;

whereas a seemly demeanour brings with it a sober and grave bearing and a cheerful attitude. I do not say that all these queer practices are great sins in themselves, nor that those who use them are great sinners in themselves; but I do say that if these queer and disordered practices govern the man who uses them to such an extent that he cannot leave them when he wishes,—then I say that they are tokens of pride and a curious mind and of a disordered display of and thirst for knowledge. And particularly they are certain tokens of instability of heart and restlessness of mind, and above all of the absence of the work of this book. This is the only reason why I set out here so many of these errors: so that the spiritual worker may test his work by them.

THE FIFTY-FOURTH CHAPTER

How by virtue of this work a man is governed by wisdom and becomes well-ordered in body and soul

Whoever possessed this work, it would govern them in a seemly manner both in body and soul, and bring them into favour with every man and woman who saw them. Even the most ill-favoured man or woman alive, if they might come by grace to work at this work, their ill-favour would suddenly and graciously be so changed that any good man who saw them would be wishful and joyful to have them in his company; and would be convinced that he was calmed in spirit and helped by grace toward God in their presence.

Whoever by grace can get this gift, let him get it. For whoever truly has it will be well able to control himself and all that belongs to him through its powers. If there were need, he would be able clearly to discern all natures and dispositions. He would be well able to make himself like all who associated with him, whether they were habitual sinners or not, without any sin in himself; all who saw him would wonder, and by the help of grace he would draw others to the work of that same spirit that he works in himself.

His demeanour and his words would be full of spiritual widsom, full of fire and fruitful; he would speak with sober certainty untainted by falsehood, very far removed from the pretence and cant of hypocrites. There are some who with all their might, inner and outer, plan how they may puff themselves up in their speech and underpin themselves on both sides to prevent falling, with many humble canting words and gestures of devotion; seeking rather to seem holy in the sight of men than to be so in the sight of God and His angels. These people will attach more importance to and be more upset about an unorthodox practice or an unsuitable or unbecoming word spoken before men, than they will be about a thousand vain thoughts and stinking impulses of sin wilfully taken upon themselves, or recklessly entertained in the sight of God, His saints and His angels in heaven. Oh Lord God! Whether or not there is any pride within when such humble canting words are so plentiful without, I can certainly grant that it is fitting and proper for him that is humble within to show humble and becoming words and gestures without, in accordance with the humility that is within his heart. But I do not say that they should be shown in broken or piping voices contrary to the disposition of those who speak them. If they are true, then let them be spoken in sincerity, with the full voice and the full spirit of him that speaks them. If he who has a clear, normal, loud voice by nature speaks poorly and pipingly,—provided that he is not sick, and that it is not between him and his God or his confessor,—then it is a true token of hypocrisy, whether the hypocrite is young or old.

What more shall I say of these venomous deceits? Really I believe, unless they have the grace to leave off this canting hypocrisy, that between the secret pride of their hearts within and such humble words without, the luckless soul will soon sink into sorrow.

THE FIFTY-FIFTH CHAPTER

*How they are mistaken who, filled with spiritual fervour,
reprove sin without discretion*

Some men the devil will deceive in the following manner.
He will inflame their brains in a very extraordinary way to
maintain God's law and to destroy sin in all other men. He
will never tempt them with a thing that is openly evil. He
makes them act like busy prelates watching over the lives of
Christian men of every degree as an abbot watches over his
monks. They will reprove everyone for their faults just as if
they had the care of their souls: yet they think they do not act
for God unless they tell others their faults that they see. They
say that they are moved to it by the fire of charity and God's
love in their hearts: but really they lie, for it is with the fire of
hell welling up in their brains and their imagination. That
this is true can be seen from the following. The devil is a
spirit, and of his own nature has no body, any more than an
angel has. Nevertheless, at any time that he or an angel shall
take on a body by God's leave, in order to minister to any
man in this life, the appearance of his bodily form to some
extent accords with the nature of the work he has to do.
Examples of this we have in the Holy Bible. Whenever an
angel was sent in bodily form in the Old Testament, and the
New Testament, too, it was always shown, either by his
name or by some organ of quality of his body, what the
spiritual matter of his message was. The devil fares in the
same way when he appears in bodily form. He shows forth
in some feature of his body what his servants are in spirit.

One example of this may be observed as covering all the
others. I have understood from some followers of necromancy who have a knowledge of how to call up wicked
spirits, and from some to whom the devil has appeared in
bodily form, that in whatever bodily form the devil appears,
he always has only one nostril, and that great and wide, and

he will gladly lift it up so that a man can see up it to the brain in his head. This brain is nothing else but hell-fire, for the devil can have no other brain: and if he can make a man look in at it he wants nothing more, for at that sight a man will lose his reason forever. But the perfect practitioner of necromancy knows this well enough and can so well arrange it therefore that the devil does him no harm.

Therefore it is as I say and have said, that always when the devil takes on any bodily shape, he shows in some feature of his body what his servants are in spirit. For he so inflames the imagination of his contemplatives with hell-fire, that suddenly without any restraint they shout out their strange conceits, and without any consideration take upon themselves to blame other men's faults too soon. This is because they have only one spiritual nostril. For the septum, which is in a man bodily and divides one nostril from the other, betokens that a man should have discretion spiritually; and can distringuish good from evil, the evil from the worse and the good from the better, before he makes final judgement about anything that he has seen or heard done or spoken around him. And by a man's brain is spiritually understood the imagination; because by nature it exists and works in the head.

THE FIFTY-SIXTH CHAPTER

How they are mistaken who rely more on their own intellectual resources, and knowledge gained in secular studies, than on the common doctrine and counsel of Holy Church

There are some who, though they are not deceived by this error that is set out here, yet on account of pride, curiosity of their natural wit and book learning, leave the common doctrine and counsel of Holy Church. These, together with all those who support them, depend too much on their own knowledge: and since they never had any grounding in this humble blind feeling and virtuous living, they deserve to have a false feeling inspired and created by their spiritual enemy. So it is that in the end he burst out and blaspheme all the saints, sacraments, laws and ordinances of Holy Church.

Sensual-living men of the world, who think that the statutes of Holy Church are too hard to be ruled by, incline to these heresies very soon and very lightly, and stoutly maintain them, because they think they will lead them an easier way than that ordained by Holy Church. Now truly I believe that those who will not go the narrow way to heaven will go the easy way to hell. Let each man test this for himself. For I believe that all such heretics and all their supporters, if they might clearly be seen as they shall be on the last day, would be seen to be heavily burdened with great and horrible secret sins of the world and their foul flesh, in addition to their open presumption in maintaining error: so that they are properly called the Antichrist's disciples. For it is said of them, that for all their false propriety in public, they are foul debauchers privately.

THE FIFTY-SEVENTH CHAPTER

How young, presumptuous disciples misunderstand the other word "up" and the errors that result from this

Enough about this for the present, and on with our subject—how these young presumptuous spiritual disciples misunderstand this other word "up".

For if it happens that either they read or have told to them that men should lift up their hearts to God, then at once they stare at the stars as if they would be above the moon, and listen in case they should hear any angels sing from heaven. These men sometimes will, in their inquisitive imagination, penetrate the planets and make a hole in the firmament to look through. These men will fashion a God according to their fancy and clothe him in rich clothes, and set him on a throne far more curious than ever was depicted on this earth. These men will create angels in bodily form and equip each one with different musical instruments far more curious than ever was seen or heard in this life.

Some of these men the devil will deceive in a singular manner, for he will send a kind of dew—they think it is angel's food—as it were coming out of the air and softly and sweetly falling into their mouths. So it is their custom to sit with their mouths gaping as if they were catching flies. Now truly, this is nothing but delusion however holy it may seem; for they have at this time souls completely empty of any true devotion. They have much vanity and falsehood in their hearts, caused by their odd manner of working; and often the devil fabricates strange sounds in their ears, strange lights shining in their eyes, and wonderful smells in their noses. All this is nothing but delusion. But they do not understand that this is so. for they think they are following the example of St. Martin looking upward and watching, when he saw by revelation God clad in his mantle amongst His angels; of St. Stephen[1] when he saw Our Lord stand in heaven, and of many others; and of Christ[2] when He ascended bodily into heaven in the sight of His disciples. Therefore they say that we should have our eyes looking upwards. I freely grant that in our bodily observance we should lift up our eyes and our hands if the spirit moves. But I do say that the work of our spirit should not be directed either upwards or downwards, or to one side or the other, or forwards or backwards, as if it were a work of the body. The reason is that our work should be spiritual not bodily, and not carried out in a bodily way.

[1] Acts VII. 55.
[2] Acts I. 9–11.

THE FIFTY-EIGHTH CHAPTER

That a man should not take St. Martin and St. Stephen as examples, nor strain his imagination bodily upwards while at prayer

As for what they say of St. Martin and St. Stephen, although they saw such things with their bodily eyes, it was shown them only as a miracle, and as attesting something spiritual. For they know perfectly well that St. Martin's mantle never was worn on Christ's body in reality, for He had no need of it to keep out the cold; but by a miracle and as a sign for all of us who can be saved, that we are united to the body of Christ in spirit. Whoever clothes a poor man, or does any other good deed for God's love bodily or spiritually to any that is in need, they may be sure that they do it to Christ spiritually; and they shall be rewarded as richly therefore as if they had done it to Christ's own body. He says this Himself in the Gospel,[1] and yet He thought that this was not enough unless He confirmed it afterwards by a miracle; and for this reason He showed Himself to St. Martin by revelation.

All the revelations that any man ever saw here in this life in bodily form have spiritual meanings. I believe that if those to whom they were shown, or we for whom they were shown, had been sufficiently spiritual, or could have understood their meaning spiritually, they would never have been shown in bodily form. Therefore let us pick off the rough husk and feed on the sweet kernel.

But how? Not as these heretics do, who may well be likened to those madmen whose custom it is, whenever they have drunk from a beautiful cup, to throw it against the wall and break it. We must not act like this if we would do well. For we should not feed on the fruit and then despise the tree, nor drink and then break the cup when we have drunk. By

[1] Matt. XXV. 40.

the tree and the cup I denote the visible miracle and all suitable bodily observance that is in accord with and does not hinder the work of the spirit. By the fruit and the drink I denote the spiritual meaning of these visible miracles and these fitting bodily observances such as the lifting of our eyes and hands to heaven. If they are done by the impulse of the spirit then they are well done, but otherwise they are hypocrisy and are false. If they are true and contain in them spiritual fruit why should they be despised? Men will kiss the cup because of the wine in it.

And what of Our Lord when He ascended into heaven made His way bodily upwards into the clouds, seen by His mother and His disciples with their bodily eyes? Should we therefore in our spiritual work always stare upwards with our bodily eyes, looking to see if we are able to see Him sitting in bodily form in heaven, or else standing, as St. Stephen saw Him? No, certainly He did not show Himself to St. Stephen in bodily form in heaven in order to give us an example that we should, in our spiritual work, look bodily up to heaven to see Him as St. Stephen did, standing or sitting or lying. For in what state His body is in heaven, standing, sitting or lying, no man knows; and it is not necessary to know this nor anything else except that His body is united with His soul without separation. His body and soul, which are His manhood, are united with the Godhead without separation also. Whether He is standing, or sitting, or lying down there is no need to know, except that He is in there as He wishes and has disposed His body in the way that is most fitting for Him. But if He shows Himself by revelation to any person in this life whether lying, standing or sitting, it is done because of some spiritual meaning, and not as being His bodily bearing in heaven.

See from the following example. By standing is understood a readiness to help. So it often happens that one friend says to another who is engaged in physical combat: "Bear yourself well, friend, and fight hard, and do not abandon the battle too easily. I will stand by you". He does not mean only actual standing, for it may be a cavalry and not an infantry battle. and it may be a running battle, not a standing one. He means when he says that he will stand by him that he will be ready to help him. It was for this reason that Our Lord showed Himself in bodily form in heaven to St. Stephen during his martyrdom, not to give us a precedent for looking up to heaven; but as if he were saying to St. Stephen as representative of all those who suffer persecution for His love: "Look, Stephen! As truly as I open the material firmament which is called heaven, and let you see me standing in bodily form, believe steadfastly that so truly I stand by you in spirit by the might of my Godhead. I am ready to help you. Therefore stand firm in the faith and suffer bravely the cruel blows of those hard stones; for I shall crown you in heaven for your reward, and not only you, but all who suffer persecution for my sake in any manner." So you can see that these bodily appearances were carrying spiritual meannings.

THE FIFTY-NINTH CHAPTER

*that a man should not take example of the bodily
ascension of Christ to strain his imagination bodily
upwards when at prayer; and that time, place and body
should all be forgotten in spiritual exercises*

If you say anything about the ascension of Our Lord, that it was done bodily with a bodily meaning as well as a spiritual one, for He ascended both true God and true man, then I will answer you as follows:— that He had been dead and was clad in immortality, and so shall we be on Judgement Day. Then we shall be made so refined both in body and soul together that we shall be where we wish bodily as swiftly as we now are in our thoughts spiritually; whether it is up or down, on one side or the other, behind or before, I believe that all will then be alike good, as the theologians say. But now you may not come to heaven bodily but spiritually—so spiritually indeed that it may not be in a bodily manner, neither upwards nor downwards nor one side nor the other nor behind nor before.

Understand that all those who set out to be spiritual workers, and especially in the work of this book, although they read "lift up" or "go in", and although the work of this book is called a stirring, yet they must pay careful attention that this stirring neither stretch up bodily nor be the sort of stirring that moves them from one place to another; and although it is sometimes called a rest they should not think of it as any such rest as implies any remaining in one place without moving from it. For the perfection of this work is so pure and spiritual in itself that if it is well and truly understood it will be seen to be far removed from any movement or any place.

It should, with some reason, rather be called a sudden changing than a movement. For time, place and body should be forgotten in all spiritual work. Therefore beware in this work of taking any example from the bodily ascension of Christ so as to strain your imagination in time of prayer bodily upwards, as if you would climb above the moon. For it could in no way be so spiritually. If you could ascend into heaven bodily as Christ did, you might take it as an example. But that may no one do but God, as He Himself bears witness, saying: "there is no man that may ascend into heaven but only He who descended from heaven, and became man for the love of man".[1] And if it were possible, as it can in no way be, then it would be for the great quantity of spiritual work wrought by the power of the spirit alone; a very long way from any bodily stressing or straining of our imagination bodily either up, or in, to one side or the other. Therefore let such falseholds alone; it could never be so.

[1] John III. 13.

91

THE SIXTIETH CHAPTER

The high road and shortest way to heaven is run by desires, not by paces of the feet

But now perhaps you say: "How can that be?". For you think that you have firm evidence that heaven is upward. For Christ ascended to it bodily upwards, and He sent the Holy Spirit as He promised coming from above bodily in the sight of all the disciples; and this is our belief. Therefore you think that because you have such firm evidence, why should you not direct you mind up bodily in time of prayer? I make you the best answer that I can, although inadequate, and say: Since it so happened that Christ should ascend bodily, and afterwards send the Holy Spirit bodily, it was more fitting that it was upwards and from above than downwards and from beneath, or behind or before, or one side or the other. But except for this fitness, He had no more need to go upwards than downwards: I mean, for the shortness of the way. For heaven spiritually is as near down as it is up, and as near up as it is down, as near behind as before, and before as behind, as near one side as the other; so that whoever had a true desire to be in heaven, at that very time he would be in heaven spiritually. For the high road and nearest road to heaven is run by desires, not by paces of the feet. Therefore St. Paul says of himself and many others: "Although our bodies are at present here on earth, our living is in heaven"[1]. He meant their love and their desire which is spiritually their life; and certainly a soul is as truly there where it loves, as in the body that lives by it and to which it gives life. And therefore, if we wish to go to heaven spiritually, there is no need to strain our spirit up or down or to one side or the other.

[1] Philippians III. 20.

THE SIXTY-FIRST CHAPTER

*That all bodily things are subject to spiritual things, and
according to the natural order, are governed by them; and
not the other way round*

Nonetheless it is necessary to lift up our hearts and eyes
bodily, as it were, to yonder bodily heaven in which the
planets are fastened. I mean if we are impelled to it by the
work of our spirit, not otherwise. For every bodily thing is
subject to a spiritual thing and ruled by it, and not the other
way round. An example of this can be seen in the Ascension
of Our Lord. For when the appointed time had come for
Him to desire to go bodily in His manhood to the Father,
from whom He was never, nor ever may be absent in the
Godhead, then mightily by the spirit of God, the manhood
with the body followed in unity of person. It was most
seemly and most fitting that the visible appearance of this
should be upwards.

The same subjection of the body to the spirit may, in a
way, be truly understood in carrying out the spiritual work
of this book, by those who work at it. For at the time the
soul settles down effectively to this work, suddenly all at
once, unknown to the person who is working, the body,
which perhaps before he began was somewhat bent to one
side or the other to ease the muscles, by the power of the
spirit will stand erect, following in bodily attitude and
appearance the work of the spirit that is carried out spiritually; and it is most proper that this should be so.

It is on account of this fitness that man, who is the noblest
creature in bodily form that God ever made, should not be
made bowed down to the earth as are all the other beasts, but
stand upright in the direction of heaven; in order to show in
bodily appearance the work of the soul spiritually, which
should be upright spiritually, and not spiritually crooked.
Take note that I say spiritually, not bodily. For how should a

soul, which has in its nature no kind of bodiliness, be drawn upright bodily? No! That cannot happen. .

Be careful, therefore, that you do not understand bodily what is meant spiritually, although it is spoken in bodily words such as these: "up" or "down", "in" or "out", "behind" or "before", "on one side or the other". For although a thing is ever so spiritual in itself, nevertheless, if it is spoken of it always has to be spoken of in bodily words, because speech is a bodily thing formed by the tongue which is an instrument of the body. What of it then? Shall it therefore be taken and understood in a bodily manner? No!—but spiritually.

THE SIXTY-SECOND CHAPTER

How a man may know when his spiritual work is beneath him or outside him, when it is level with him or within him, and when it is above him and under God.

So that you may know better how to understand spiritually those words which are spoken bodily, I have decided to explain to you the spiritual meaning of some words that pertain to spiritual work; so that you may know clearly without any mistake when your spiritual work is beneath you and outside you, when it is within you and level with you and when it is above you and under God.

Every kind of bodily thing is outside your soul and beneath it by nature. Yes! The sun, the moon and all the stars, although they are above your body, nevertheless they are beneath your soul. All the angels and all souls, although they may be confirmed and adorned with grace and virtue and therefore be above you in purity, they are nevertheless only level with you by nature. Within you by nature are the powers of your soul, of which the three principal ones are mind, reason and will; and the secondary ones imagination and sensuality.

By nature there is nothing at all above you but only God alone.

Whenever you find "yourself" written in spiritual writing, then it means your soul, not your body. Then according to the thing on which the powers of your soul work, so shall the worth and condition of your work be judged; whether it is beneath you, within you, or above you.

THE SIXTY-THIRD CHAPTER

Of the powers of the soul in general and especially how the memory is the principal power, comprehending in itself all the other powers and their activities

Memory is a kind of power that, properly and accurately, does not itself work. But reason and will are two working powers, and so are imagination and sensuality. All these four powers and their actions memory contains and comprehends in itself; and in no way can it be said to work unless such comprehension is work.

It is for this reason that I call some of the powers of the soul "principal", some "secondary"; not that the soul is divisible; for that cannot be, but because all the things in which they work are divisible; some principal, as are all spiritual things, some secondary, as are all bodily things. The two principal working powers, reason and will, work entirely by themselves in all spiritual things without the help of the two secondary powers. Imagination and sensuality work at an animal level with all bodily things, whether they are present or absent, in the body and with bodily intelligence. But through these alone, without the help of reason, a soul may never come to know the condition of bodily creatures, nor the cause of their being and their making.

Because of this, reason and will are called principal powers; that they work in pure spirit without any trace of the bodily: and imagination and sensuality secondary,

because they work in the body with bodily instruments—
these are our five wits. Memory is called the principal power
because it contains in itself spiritually not only all other
powers but also all the things in which they work. Learn this
be experience.

THE SIXTY-FOURTH CHAPTER

*Of the two other principal powers, reason and will, and
of their work before and after sin*

Reason is the power through which we distinguish evil from
good, bad from worse, good from better, worse from
worst, and better from best. Before man sinned, reason
might have done this by nature; but now it is so blinded by
original sin that it cannot do this work unless it is illumined
by grace. Both reason in itself, and the thing that it works at
are comprehended and contained in the mind.

Will is the power by which we choose good, after it has
been determined by reason; and through which we love
God, desire God and finally rest with complete pleasure and
full consent in God. Before man sinned, will could not be at
fault in its choosing, in its loving, or in any of its works,
because it could then by nature appreciate each thing as it
was. But now it cannot do so unless it is anointed with grace.
For often, because of the infection of original sin, it esteems a
thing good which is very evil, and that has but the
appearance of goodness. The memory contains in itself both
the will and the thing that is willed.

THE SIXTY-FIFTH CHAPTER

*Of the first secondary power, named imagination; and of
its works and its obedience to reason, before and after sin*

Imagination is the power through which we portray all
images of things present and absent. Both it and the thing

hat it works at are contained in the memory. Before man
inned, imagination was obedient to reason, to which it was
s it were servant: so that it never presented to it any dis-
rderly image of any bodily creature, nor any fantasy of any
piritual creature.

But now it is not so. Unless it is restrained by the light of
grace in the reason, it will never cease, sleeping or waking,
o portray various disordered images of bodily creatures; or
lse some fantasy which is nothing else than a bodily con-
eption of something spiritual, or a spiritual conception of
omething bodily. This is always fabricated, false, and akin
o error. The disobedience of the imagination may be clearly
perceived in them that are newly turned from the world to
devotion, at the time of their prayer. For, before the time
comes when the imagination has been restrained for the
most part by the light of grace in the reason,—as it is by
continual meditation on spiritual things such as their own
wretchedness, the passion and kindness of Our Lord God,
and many other such things,—they are in no way able to put
aside the extraordinary and various thoughts, fantasies and
images which are ministered and imprinted in their minds
by the light and the curiosity of imagination. All this disobedience is the penalty of original sin.

THE SIXTY-SIXTH CHAPTER

Of the other secondary power, named sensuality, and of
its works and its obedience to the will, before and after sin

Sensuality is the power of our soul affecting and controlling
our bodily senses, through which we have bodily knowledge and feeling of all bodily creatures, whether pleasurable
or vexatious. It has two parts; one through which it sees to
the needs of our bodies, and another through which it serves
the desires of the bodily senses. For the same power is the
one which complains when the body is without things it

needs, and in the satisfying of the need stirs us up to tak
more than is needed in order to feed and further ou
appetites. It grumbles at the absence of things that please i
and is inordinately delighted when they are there. It grum
bles at the presence of things it dislikes and is inordinatel
pleased at their absence. Both this power and its work ar
contained in the mind.

Before man sinned, sensuality was so obedient to the will
whose servant, so to speak, it is, that it never suggested to i
any disorderly pleasure or complaint in respect of any bodil
creature, nor any spiritual pretence of liking or dislikin
induced by any spiritual enemy in the bodily senses. Bu
now it is not so. For unless it is directed by grace in the wi
to suffer humbly and temperately the penalty of original sin
which it feels in the absence of comforts it needs and in th
presence of discomforts beneficial to it; and moreover, t
refrain from lust at the presence of comforts it needs, an
from inordinate pleasure at the absence of discomforts bene
ficial to it; it will wretchedly and wantonly wallow, like
swine in the mire, in the riches of this world and the fou
flesh, so that our whole mode of life will be more bestial an
fleshly than human and spiritual.

THE SIXTY-SEVENTH CHAPTER

*That anyone who does not know the powers of the soul
and the manner of its working may easily be mistaken in
understanding spiritual words and spiritual working; and
how a soul is made a God through grace*

See, spiritual friend! To such wretchedness as here you ma
see are we fallen through sin. What wonder is it then that w
are blindly and easily led astray in understanding spiritua
words and spiritual work, and especially those who do no
yet know the powers of the soul and the way they work?

Whenever the mind is occupied by something bodily, t

however good an end it may lead, nevertheless you are beneath yourself in this work and outside your soul. And whenever you feel your mind occupied with the subtle conditions of the powers of your soul and their work in spiritual things—for example, the vices and virtues of yourself or any other creatuure that is spiritual and equal to you in nature—to the end that you may by this work learn to know yourself in order to advance towards perfection; then you are within yourself and level with yourself. But whenever you feel your mind occupied with nothing at all that is bodily or spiritual, but only with the very substance of God, as it is and may be in the practice of the work of this book, then you are above yourself and under your God.

You are above yourself because you have managed to come by grace whither you could not come by nature; that is to say, to be united with God in spirit, love and accordance of will. You are beneath your God because, although it may be said in a manner of speaking that you and your God are not two, but one in spirit—so that you, or another who feels the perfection of this work on account of this union, may truthfully as the scriptures witness[1] be called a god; nevertheless you are still beneath Him. This is because He is God by nature without any beginning; and you, who at one time were nothing in substance, and who moreover when by His might and love you were made something, wilfully by sin made yourself less than nothing; only by His undeserved mercy are you made a god by grace, united with Him in spirit without separation, both here and in the bliss of heaven without end. So that although you are altogether one with Him by grace, you are very far beneath Him in nature.

My spiritual friend, here you may see in some part that whoever does no know the powers of his own soul, and how

[1] Psalms 82 (81): verse 6.
John X. 34.

they work, may very easily be mistaken in understanding words written with a spiritual intent. And hence you may see something of the reason why I did not dare bid you show openly your desire to God, but bid you childishly do what you could to hide it and conceal it. This I do for fear that you should understand bodily what is meant spiritually.

THE SIXTY-EIGHTH CHAPTER

That nowhere bodily is everywhere spiritually, and how our outward man deems the work of this book of no account

And in the same manner, where another man would tell you to gather your power and your wits wholly within yourself and worship God there—although in this he speaks very well and truly, yes indeed, and no man more truly if he is properly understood—yet I do not wish to bid you do so for fear of misunderstanding and a bodily interpretation of his words. But I advise you as follows: look to it that you be in no way within yourself, and to put it shortly I do not want you to be outside yourself, nor above, nor below, nor on one side or the other.

"Where should I be, then?" you say. "Nowhere, by your account". Now indeed you are speaking well, for this is where I would have you be, because nowhere bodily is everywhere spiritually. So look to it carefully that your spiritual work is nowhere bodily. Then wherever the thing is that you work on deliberately in the substance of your mind, certainly you are there in spirit as truly as your body is in that place where you are bodily; and although your bodily senses can find nothing to feed on there—for they think that your are doing nothing,—yes!; carry on with this nothing and do it for the love of God. Do not stop at all for that, but work hard at that nothing with a vigilant desire in your will to have God whom no man can know. For I tell you truly, I would rather be thus nowhere bodily, wrestling with that blind nothing, than to be so great a lord that I might when I wished be everywhere bodily, merely playing with all this something as a lord with his own property.

Let this everywhere and this something alone in exchange for this nowhere and this nothing. Do not bother if your senses can have no understanding of this nothing; for this I love it all the better. It is such a valuable thing in itself that they cannot understand it. This nothing may better be felt than seen, for it is very obscure and very dark to those who have looked on it for only a little while. Nevertheless, if I am to speak more truly, a soul is more blinded in feeling for it by superabundance of spiritual light than by any darkness or lack of bodily light. Who is he that calls it nothing? Certainly our outer man, not our inner. Our inner man calls it All; for through it he has been taught how to understand all things, bodily and spiritual, without any special attention to any one thing in itself.

THE SIXTY-NINTH CHAPTER

How a man's disposition is marvellously changed in the spiritual feeling of this nought when it is nowhere wrought

A man's disposition is wonderfully changed in the spiritual feeling of this nought when it is nowhere wrought. For the first time he looks at it he will find all his particular deeds of sin that he has ever committed since he was born, bodily or spiritual, secretly or darkly, printed on it. However he turns it about, they will always appear before his eyes until the time when with much hard labour, much sore sighing, and many bitter tears he has for the most part rubbed them away. Sometimes in this labour he thinks that looking on it is like looking on hell, for he thinks that he has no hope of winning to the perfection of spiritual rest out of that pain.

There are many who come this far inward, but because of the greatness of the pain that they feel and the absence of comfort, they go back to regarding bodily things, seeking fleshly comforts outside for lack of the spiritual comforts that they have not yet deserved, but would deserve if they had persevered.

For he that perseveres sometimes feels some comfort, and has some hope of perfection; for he feels and sees that many of his former particular sins have by the help of grace for the most part been rubbed away. Nevertheless he is still constantly feeling pain, but he believes it will have an end as it grows ever less and less, and therefore he calls it not hell but purgatory.

Sometimes he can find no special sin written on it, and then he thinks that sin is a lump, he knows not of what, nothing but himself; and this may be called the stump and the pain or original sin. Sometimes he thinks that it is paradise or heaven, because of the wonderful delights and comforts, joys and blessed virtues that he finds there. Sometimes he thinks that it is God, because of the peace and rest that he finds there. Indeed, let him think what he will; he will always find it a cloud of unknowing that is between him and his God.

THE SEVENTIETH CHAPTER

That even as by weakening our bodily wit we begin most readily to come to the knowledge of spiritual things, so by the weakening of our spiritual wits we begin most readily to come to the knowledge of God, as far as it is possible by grace to know Him here

Therefore work hard at this nought and this nowhere, and abandon your outward bodily senses and all that they work in: for I tell you truly, this work cannot be understood by them.

For by your eyes you cannot understand anything except in its length or breadth, smallness or greatness, roundness or squareness, farness or nearness, and its colour. By your ears nothing but noise or some kind of sound, by your nose nothing but stench or scent; by your taste nothing but sweet or sour, salt or fresh, bitter or pleasant; by your feeling nothing but hot or cold, hard or soft, blunt or sharp. And truly neither God nor spiritual things have any of these qualities or quantities. Therefore, leave your outward senses and work with them neither within nor without. For all those who set out to be spiritual workers within, and think they either hear, smell, see, taste or feel spiritual things either within them or outside, most certainly are deceived and work wrongly against the course of nature. For by nature it is ordained that through the senses man should gain knowledge of all outward bodily things, but in no way come to the knowledge of spiritual things: not, I mean, by their work. By their failure we may: for example, when we read about certain things, or hear them spoken about and understand that our outer senses cannot tell us by any quality what these things are, we can be quite sure that these things are spiritual and not bodily.

In the same way spiritually it happens to our spiritual senses when we strive after the knowledge of God Himself. For although a man may have ever so much spiritual understanding in the knowledge of spiritual created things, yet he can never by the work of his understanding come to the knowledge of an unmade spiritual thing, which is nothing else but God. But by its failure he may, because that thing in which it fails is nothing else but God alone.

Therefore it was that St. Denis says: "The very best way of knowing God is that which is known by unknowing". Whoever consults Denis' books will find that his words clearly confirm all that I have said or shall say from the beginning of this treatise to the end. Except in this one place I have no wish to quote him or any other authority at this time. For of old, men thought it a sign of humility to say nothing out of their own heads unless it was confirmed by the scripture or the words of a doctor of the Church; but now this has turned into ingenuity and a display of learning. For you this is needless and therefore I do not do it. Whoever has ears let him hear, and whoever is stirred up to believe let him believe. Otherwise they will not.

THE SEVENTY-FIRST CHAPTER

That some may feel the perfection of this work only in time of ecstasy, and some may have it when they will in the common state of man's soul

Some people think this matter so hard and so awesome that they say it may not be obtained without much hard toil coming first, and that it can be conceived but seldom, and that in time of ecstasy. To these men I reply, though inadequately, and say that it is all at the ordinance and disposition of God, according to the spiritual capabilities of those to whom the grace of contemplation and spiritual working is given. There are some who cannot come to it without great and lengthy spiritual exercises; and even then it will be very seldom and at the special calling of Our Lord that they will feel the perfection of the work. This is called ecstasy. Some there are, so refined in grace and spirit, and so familiar with God in the grace of contemplation, that they are able to have it whenever they wish in the common state of man's soul,— sitting, moving, standing or kneeling. Yet at the same time they have full control of all their faculties, bodily and spiritual, and are able to use them if they wish; not without some difficulty, but without great difficulty. An example of this first we have in Moses; of the other in Aaron, the priest of the temple.

For the grace of contemplation is represented by the Ark of the Covenant in the old law, and the workers in this grace are represented by those who had most to do around the Ark, as the story bears witness. And this grace and this work are rightly likened to the Ark. For just as that Ark contained all the jewels and relics of the Temple, even so the little love set upon the cloud of unknowing contains all the virtues of man's soul, which is the spiritual temple of God.

Moses, before he might see the Ark and learn how it should be made, had with much toil to climb up to the top of the mountain: he dwelt there and worked in a cloud for six days, waiting until the seventh when Our Lord would deign to show him the manner in which the Ark should be made. By Moses' long labour and his late revelation are understood those that are not able to come to perfection of this spiritual work without a long period of hard toil coming first; and then but seldom and when God deigns to show it.

But though Moses might come and see it very seldom and not without long and hard toil, Aaron had it in his power, because of his office, to see it in the Temple within the veil as often as he wished to enter. And by this Aaron are understood all those that I spoke about above, who through their spiritual intelligence, by the help of grace, are able to make the perfection of this work their own as often as they like.

THE SEVENTY-SECOND CHAPTER

That one who takes part in this work should not suppose nor judge that anyone else engaged in it has the same experience as himself

Now by this you may see that he who cannot attain to seeing and feeling the perfection of this work without much toil, and then only seldom, may easily be mistaken if he speaks, judges or thinks of other men in terms of his own experience; that they can only come to it very occasionally, and that not without great toil.

In the same way the man may be mistaken who has it

when he will, if he judges all others according to his own experience, saying that they are able to have it when they will. Let this alone: for surely he cannot think like that. For perhaps, when it pleases God, though at first they can only have it occasionally, and that not without great toil, afterwards they shall have it when they will, as often as they like. We have an example of this in Moses who at first might see the form of the Ark but seldom and not without great toil on the mountain: but afterwards saw it in the valley as often as he liked.

THE SEVENTY-THIRD CHAPTER

That in a similar manner to Moses, Aaron and Bezaleel busy about the Ark of the Covenant, we profit in three ways from the grace of contemplation, for this grace is prefigured by the Ark.

There were three men who principally busied themselves with this Ark of the Old Testament: Moses, Bezaleel and Aaron.[1] Moses learnt of Our Lord on the mountain how it should be made. Bezaleel worked at it and made it in the valley according to the pattern which was revealed on the mountain. Aaron had care of it in the Temple, and was able to see it and feel it as often as he liked. In a similar manner to these three we profit in three ways in the grace of contemplation. Sometimes we profit only by grace, and then we are like Moses, who in spite of all the climbing and toil that he had on the mountain, might come and see it only occasionally; and even then that sight was only by revelation of Our Lord when it pleased Him to reveal it, not as any reward for his toil. Sometimes we profit in this grace by our own spiritual reasoning supported by grace, and then we are like Bezaleel, who could not see the Ark until he had made it

---

[1] Exodus XXIV. 15 ff.

by his own labour, with the help of the pattern that was shown to Moses on the mountain. Sometimes we profit in this grace through other men's teaching, and then we are like Aaron, who had in his charge the Ark which Bezaleel had constructed and given ready made into his hands, and could feel it and see it whenever he wished.

Spiritual friend, you see that in this work—although it is childishly and uncouthly spoken—I bear the office of Bezaleel, although I am a wretch and unworthy to teach any creature—making this spiritual Ark and declaring its nature in a way that you may find useful. But you must work far better and more worthily than I do if you will be Aaron: that is to say, continually working therein for yourself and for me. Do so I pray you for the love of Almighty God; and since we are both called by God to labour in this work, I beg you for the love of God to fulfil on your part what is lacking on mine.

THE SEVENTY-FOURTH CHAPTER

How the substance of this book may never be read nor spoken about, nor heard read or spoken about, by a soul well disposed to it, without a feeling of real agreement with the purpose of this work: and a repetition of the order that was given in the prologue

If you think that this manner of working is not according to your disposition in body and soul, you may leave it and take another in safety with good spiritual counsel, and no blame is attached to you. Then I beseech you that you will hold me excused, for truly I would have benefitted you in this writing with my simple knowledge, and that was my intention. Therefore, read it over two or three times, the more often the better, and the more of it you will understand; indeed it may be that some clause that was very hard for you to understand at the first and second readings, soon after you will find very easy.

Indeed, it seems to my mind impossible that any soul that is disposed to this work should read or speak of it, or else hear it read or spoken of, without that same soul feeling for the time being a complete accord with the purpose of this work. Then, if you think it does you good, thank God heartily, and for God's love pray for me.

Do this then, and I pray you by God's love that you let no-one see this book unless you think he is a suitable person to make use of it, in accordance with what you find written in the book, where it tells you what men should work at this work, and when. If you let any such men see it, then I pray you bid them take their time to read it right through, for perhaps there is something in it, at the beginning or in the middle, which is left hanging in the air and not explained where it stands. But if it is not explained there it will be soon after or else in the end. So if anyone saw one part and not another, perhaps he could easily be led into error; and therefore I pray you to do as I tell you.

If you think that there is anything in the book that you would like to have explained more clearly than it is, let me know what it is, and your understanding of it; and as far as my simple knowledge goes, I will clarify it if I can.

As to worldly chatterers, flatterers, disparagers, whisperers and tale-bearers and all kinds of carping critics, I would not care at all if they never saw this book: for it was never my intention to write such a book for them. I would rather that they did not hear it, neither they, nor those acting purely out of curiosity, whether men of letters or illiterates. Yes; even though they may be very good men in their daily life, there is nothing in it for them.

THE SEVENTY-FIFTH CHAPTER

*Of some sure indications whereby a man may verify
whether he is called by God to this work*

All those who read or hear the substance of this book read or
spoken about, and when hearing or reading it think that it is
a good and desirable thing, are not on that account called by
God to labour at this work, just because of that pleasant
impulse that they feel at the time of reading. For perhaps this
impulse comes more from natural curiosity of the intellect
than from any calling of grace.

But if they would test whence this impulse comes, they
can test it like this if they want to. First let them check if they
have done all that they can beforehand to make themselves
capable of it, by cleansing their conscience according to the
judgement of Holy Church with the agreement of their
Director. If this is so, then so far all is well. But if they wish
to know more surely, let them check if this is always pressing upon their minds more habitually than any other spiritual exercise, and if they think that there is nothing that they
do bodily or spiritually that is of sufficient value according
to their conscience unless this secret little love set upon the
cloud of unknowing is in a spiritual way the chief thing of all
their work. If they feel like this, then it is a sign that they are
called by God to this work, and certainly otherwise they are
not.

I do not say that it will always last and dwell continually in
the minds of those called to do this work. No, this is not so.
For the actual feeling is often withdrawn from the young
spiritual apprentice in this work, for various reasons. Sometimes so that he may not presume too much on it, and think
that it is for the most part in his power to have it as and when
he wishes. Such a thought would be pride. Always when the
feeling of this grace is withdrawn the cause is pride; not
always pride that actually is, but pride that would be were

not the feeling of grace withdrawn. And so some young fools often think that God is their enemy when He is their complete friend.

Sometimes it is withdrawn because of carelessness, and when this happens they feel a bitter pain that racks them very sorely. Sometimes Our Lord delays it on purpose, for He would by such a delay make it grow, and be held in more esteem when that which has been lost for a long time is new found and felt again. And this is one of the readiest and most sovereign signs that a soul may have to know whether he is called to work this work; if he feels, after such a delay and long absence of this work, that when it comes suddenly as it does, not achieved through any act of his, that he has then a greater fervour of desire and a greater love-longing to work at this work than ever he had at any time before—and indeed I believe he has often more joy in finding it than ever he had sorrow at losing it.

If it is like this, it is a truly infallible sign that he is called by God to work at this work, whatever he is or has been. For God, with His merciful eyes does not regard what you are or what you have been, but what you would be. St. Gregory[1] is witness that: "All holy desires grow by delays, and if they wane by delays then they were never holy desires". For if a man always feels less and less joy at the finding anew and sudden offering of desires he has previously formed, although these may be called natural desires for what is good, nonetheless they never were holy desires. Of this holy desire St. Augustine[2] speaks and says: "The life of a good Christian man is nothing else but holy desire."

Farewell, spiritual friend, with God's blessing and mine: and I beseech Almighty God that true peace, holy counsel and spiritual comfort in God, with abundance of grace, be evermore with you and all God's lovers on earth.   Amen.

[1] Gregory the Great: Homilia in Evangelia II. 25.
[2] St. Augustine: In Epistolam Joannis ad Parthos IV. 6.

THE LETTER OF
PRIVATE DIRECTION

THE LETTER OF PRIVATE DIRECTION
Prologue

Spiritual friend in God, as touching the inward calling to which I believe you are disposed. I am speaking this time for your ears alone and not for everyone in general who should happen to see what is written. For if I were writing for everybody, then I must write what is applicable to everybody in general. This time I am writing specially to you. Therefore I shall not write anything except such things as I think most helpful and concerned with your condition. If there is anyone else feeling as you do to whom this work may be profitable as it is to you, so much the better: I am well pleased. Nevertheless, at this time your own inward condition as I understand it is alone, by itself, the aim and target of my consideration. Therefore I say this to you as representative of all others like you.

THE FIRST CHAPTER

When you enter into a state of recollection do not think beforehand what you will do afterwards, but forsake good thoughts as well as evil ones. Do not pray in words unless you have a strong desire to do so. Then, if you do say anything, do not consider how long or how short it is, nor attach any importance to what it is or what it means, whether it is a prayer, a psalm, a hymn, anthem or any other act of devotion general or special, either mentally within, composed in thought, or vocally without, by the use of words. Only look to it that nothing remains in the working of your mind but a simple desire reaching towards God, not clothed in any special thought of God's nature or any of His works, but only that He is. Let Him be like this I beg you, and do not form Him in any other manner. Seek no further for Him by the ingenuity of your mind. Let that be the foundation of your belief. This simple desire, freely fastened and founded on true belief, will be nothing else in your thought and feeling but a simple thought and blind feeling of your own being, as if you said to God inside yourself something like this: "What I am, Lord, I offer to you, without any regard to any attribute of Your being, but only that You are as you are, and nothing else".

Let that humble darkness be your mirror and occupy the whole of your mind. Think no more of yourself than I bid you think of your God, so that you may be one with Him in spirit without any separation or disturbance of the mind. He is your being, and in Him you are what you are, not only by origin and being, but also He is in you as both your origin and your being. Think of God in this work as you do of yourself and of yourself as you do of God, that He is as He is, and you are as you are, so that your thought may not be disturbed or separated, but united with Him that is all, excepting always the difference between you and Him, that He is your being and you are not His. For although all things are in Him as their origin and their being, yet in Himself alone, He is His own origin and His own being.

For as nothing can be without Him, so He cannot be without Himself. He is being both to Himself and to all. And He alone is separated from the all, in that He is the being both of Himself and all. And He is united in all and all in Him, for all things have their beginnings in Him, and He is the being of all. In this way, your thought and your feeling will be indissolubly united with Him in grace, and all speculative searching for the abstruse qualities of your secret being, or His, put far from you so that your thought is simple and your feelings in no way contaminated: then you yourself, stripped of everything, just as you are, by the touch of grace will be secretly fed in your feelings only with Him as He is. This will be only blindly and in part, as is all that can happen here in this life, so that your longing desire may always be working.

THE LETTER OF PRIVATE DIRECTION

Look up joyously and say to your Lord, either out loud or meaning it in your heart: "What I am I offer you, for it is You". Think simply, plainly and unashamedly that you are as you are without speculating further. This seems to me easy to understand if it were asked of the most uncultured man or woman alive with the most ordinary state of natural intelligence. Therefore quietly, with a sad smile, I am astonished when I hear some men (I do not mean simply unlearned men and women, but scholars and men of great learning) say that what I write to you and to others is so hard and so elevated, so speculative and so unusual, that it can scarcely be understood by the cleverest scholar or the most intelligent man or woman alive. So they say, but I reply to them that it is rightly a cause of much sorrow and a thing to be mercifully rejected and bitterly reproved by God and those who love Him, that nowadays, not only a few people but nearly all generally (if we except one or two in each district who are especially chosen by God) are blinded by their speculative knowledge, acquired and natural: and so this easy work, through which the souls of the most uncultured men and women are truly, in loving humility, united with God in perfect love, can no more—indeed, not as much—be truly understood by them in certainty of spirit, on account of their blindness and speculation, than the knowledge of the greatest scholar in the university can be understood by a young child learning his A B C. Owing to this blindness, they mistakenly call such simple teaching "speculation": whereas, if it is examined intelligently, it will be found to be a simple and easy lesson for an unlearned man.

I hold him worse than unlearned and uncultivated who cannot think and feel that he himself exists, not what he is, but that he is. For to feel its own proper existence is plainly in the power of the most unknowledgeable cow and most unreasonable beast—(if it could be said, as it cannot, that one is more unknowledgeable or more unreasonable than

115

another). Much more, then, is it in the power of man, who is singularly endowed with reason beyond all other beasts, to think and feel his own proper being.

Come down then to the lowest point of your intelligence which some men hold from actual experience to be the highest, and think in the most ignorant manner which some men consider to be the wisest, not what you yourself are, but that you yourself are. For to think what you are in all your characteristics requires great expertise in scholarship and learning, and much careful searching of your natural intelligence: and this you have now done for a long time, with the help of grace. So that you know something, and as much as I think it is profitable for you to know at this time, of what you are;—a man by nature, and a foul stinking wretch through sin. How well you know it! Perhaps sometimes you think you know too well all the filth that pursues and falls upon a wretch. Fie on them! Let it alone, I pray you. Don't stir it up any more for fear of the stink. But you can, in spite of your ignorance and uncouthness, without any great knowledge of scholarship or natural intelligence, think that you exist.

THE SECOND CHAPTER

Therefore I pray you, do no more in the matter but think unashamedly that you are as you are, however foul and wretched you may be; provided that before this you have lawfully obtained pardon for all your sins habitual and general, in accordance with the true teaching of holy Church, (as I suppose you have). For otherwise neither you nor any other shall with my consent be so bold as to take on this work. But if you feel that you have done all that you can, then you should undertake this work, although you still feel yourself so vile and wretched, and that you are such a hindrance to yourself, that you do not know what is best for

ou to do with yourself. You must still do as I tell you. Take
good gracious God as He is and lay Him like a poultice on
your sick self as you are; or, to put it otherwise, lift up your
sick self just as you are, and strive by your longing to touch
good gracious God as He is: for in touching Him there is
endless health as the woman in the Gospel bears witness
saying "If I can but touch the hem of His garment I shall be
healed".[1] Much more will you be healed of your sickness by
the high heavenly touch of His own being, His own dear
self. Step up boldly then, and taste this elixir. Raise up your
sick self as you are to gracious God as He is, without any
speculative or particular consideration of any at all of the
qualities that belong to your being or to God's, whether they
are pure or corrupted, sprung from grace or nature, divine
or human. The only thing that matters to you now is that the
unseeing awareness of your bare being be gladly borne up in
the eager longing of love to be united in grace and spirit to
the precious being of God in Himself, alone as He is without
anything else. And if your undisciplined enquiring senses
can find no nourishment in this form of action, and therefore
will always grumble and bid you leave the work and do
some good in their speculative way,—(for it seems to them
that what you are doing is of no value because they have no
knowledge of it),—why, then I should be the better pleased,
because so it is shown to be of more value than they are. And
why should I not be better pleased, since there is nothing
that I can do, nor that can be fashioned in the speculation of
my senses, bodily or spiritual, that might bring me so near
to God and so far from the world as this simple little feeling
and the offering up of my blind being would do?

Therefore, although your senses can find no nourishment
in this work and therefore would have you go from it, see
that you do not leave it for them, but you be their master and
do not go back to feed them however mad they may be. You

[1] Matthew IX. 21.

go back to feed your senses when you allow them to seek out in various speculative mediations the qualities of your being. These meditations, although they may be very good and profitable, are, in comparison with the blind feeling and offering of your being, very diffuse and destructive of the perfection of unity that should be between God and your soul. Therefore, hold yourself in the first point of the spirit which is your being, and do not go back for anything, however good and holy the thing may seem into which your senses would lead you.

THE THIRD CHAPTER

Carry out the teaching and counsel of Solomon who said to his son:[1] "Honour the Lord with your substance, and with your first fruits feed the poor; so your barns will be filled with plenty and your presses will overflow with wine". This is the lesson that Solomon gave to his son bodily, but as it were meaning you to understand it spiritually, and so I shall pass it on to you in his name: "My spiritual friend in God, make sure that leaving all speculative searching in your natural senses you give yourself wholly to the worship of God with your substance, offering Him simply and wholly your own self, all that you are, and such as you are, but in a general not in a special way, (that is without any special attention to what you are), so that your looking be not dissipated nor your feeling befouled; which would make you less united with God in purity of spirit. You are to feed the poor with your first fruits, that is with the first of your spiritual and bodily qualities which have grown up with you from the very beginning of your creation to this day."

I call your fruits all the gifts of nature and grace that God gave you at any time; with which it is your duty to foster and

[1] Proverbs III. 9, 10.

118

feed in this life both bodily and spiritually, all your brothers and sisters through nature and through grace in the same way as you do yourself. The first of these gifts I call your first fruits. The first gift to each creature is nothing else than the being of that creature. For although the qualities of your being are so firmly united to the being itself that they are inseparable, yet since they all depend on it it may truly be called, as it is, the first of the gifts. And so it is only your being that is the first of your fruits. For if you extend the speculative consideration of your heart to any or to all of the complex qualties and worthwhile characteristics that belong to the being of man,—who is the noblest being of all things made,—you will always find that the first target and aim of your consideration, whatever it may be, is your bare being.

It is as if you said to yourself in each one of your considerations,—stirring yourself up by means of this consideration to the love and praise of your God, who gave you not only being but such a noble being as the qualities of your life will witness in the course of your considerations,—as if you said: "I am, I see and feel that I am, and not only I am, but I am this, and this, and this",—reckoning, during your consideration, all the special qualities of your being. Then,—the most important step of all—wrap it all up together and say as follows: "What I am and how I am by nature and by grace, I have it all from you and it is You. I offer it all to You, chiefly to praise You, and to help all my fellow Christians and myself". And so you may see that the first target of your consideration is most substantially in the bare and blind feeling of your own being; and so it is only your being that is your first fruit.

But although it is the first of all your fruits and therefore all the other fruits depend on it, it is no profit at present to wrap or clothe your consideration of it in any or all the sutble qualities of it which I call the fruits, and at which you had been working before this. It is enough now that you wholly worship God with your substance, and offer up your bare being, which is your first fruit, as a continual sacrifice of praise to God both for yourself and all others, as love demands; not clothing it with any characteristic, or any special consideration that in any way pertains or may pertain to the being of yourself or any other,—as if you would by that consideration help the need, further the well-being, or increase the progress in perfection of yourself or someone else.

Let this alone, for truly it will have no such effect in this case. The blind general consideration will give more help to the need, well-being and perfecting of yourself and all others in purity of spirit than any special consideration that any man may have, however, holy it seems.

That this is true is witnessed by the scriptures, by the example of Christ, and by common sense. For as all men fell in Adam, because he fell from this unifying love; and as all who with fidelity to their calling, bear witness to their desire for salvation, are saved—and shall be by the power of the Passion of Christ alone. For Christ in the truest sacrifice offered all that He was in general and not for a special purpose, without any particular regard to any man alive, but generally and universally for all: even so, a man who truly and perfectly sacrifices himself for the general good of all does all that he can to bind all men to God as effectively as he himself is bound. And no greater act of love may any man do than thus to sacrifice himself for all his brothers and sisters in nature and grace. For as the soul is of more worth than the body, so the binding of the soul to God its life by the heavenly food of love is better than the binding of the body to the soul its life by any earthly food in this life. The latter is a good thing to do for its own sake, but without the former it is never well done. The two together are better; but the former by itself is best. The second by itself never merits salvation; but the first by itself, when the full measure of the second fails, not only merits salvation, but leads to the greatest perfection.

THE FOURTH CHAPTER

There is no need now, in order that you may increase your perfection, to go back to feed your senses, as happens when you consider the qualities of your being, so that you may by such considerations feed and fill your affections with loving and pleasant feeling for God and spiritual things, and your understanding with spiritual wisdom from meditations in search of the knowledge of God.

For if you hold yourself diligently, as you may by grace, always and continuously in the first aim of your spirit offering up to God that bare blind feeling of your own being, which I call your first fruits; then you can be certain that the latter part of Solomon's lesson will truly be fulfilled as he promises, without any trouble to yourself of searching and rummaging with your spiritual senses among any of the qualities that belong not only to your own being but to the being of God.

For you must thoroughly understand in this work you shall have no more consideration about the qualities of God's being than about the qualities of you own being. For there is no name, nor feeling nor consideration either more or indeed as much in accord with the eternity which is God as that which can be seen and felt in the blind loving consideration of the word "Is". For if you say "Good" or "Fair Lord" or "Sweet", "Merciful" or "Righteous", "Wise" or "Omniscient", "Mighty" or "Omnipotent", "Knowledge" or "Wisdom", "Might" or "Strength", "Love" or "Charity", or any other such thing that you wish to say of God; all is hidden and contained in the little word "Is". For to be is to Him to be all these things, and if you added a hundred thousand sweet words such as these—"Good", "Fair" and all the rest, you have not departed from the little word "Is". And if you say them all, you have not added to it, and if you do not say one you have not diminished it.

THE LETTER OF PRIVATE DIRECTION

Therefore, be as blind in the loving consideration of the being of your God as in the simple consideration of you own being without any speculative searching in your senses to look for any quality that belongs to His being or to yours. But with all speculation left behind and put far from you, give worship to your God with your substance, all that you are as you are to all of Him as He is, who alone by Himself without anything else is the blessed being both of Himself and of you. Thus you shall unitively and in a marvellous manner worship God with Himself, since that which you are you have from Him, and it is He.

For although you had a beginning when your substance was created,—which was at one time nothing,—yet you have always existed in Him without any beginning, and always shall without ending, as God Himself is. Therefore I often cry out, and always this one thing: "Worship your God with your substance and give common benefit to all men with your first fruits; then shall your barns be filled with plenty". That is: "Then shall your spiritual feelings be filled with the fullness of love and virtuous living in God your foundation, the purifier of your spirit". "And your wine-presses will overflow with wine". That is: your inward spiritual senses, which you are accustomed to strain and press together by various speculative meditations and rational investigations into the spiritual knowledge of God and yourself, as you consider His qualities and yours, shall then overflow with wine, by which wine, in Holy Scripture, is truly and mystically understood spiritual wisdom in true contemplation and lofty savouring of the Godhead.

All this will happen suddenly, joyously, and through grace, without any trouble or toil on your part, simply by the ministration of angels, through the power of this blind loving work. For all the angels' knowledge does special service to it as the maidservant to her mistress.[1]

[1] See Psalm 123 (122): verse 2.

THE FIFTH CHAPTER

In great commendation of this joyous simple work, which is in itself the high wisdom of the Godhead graciously descending into man's soul, binding and uniting it with Himself in spiritual wisdom and discernment, the wise Solomon bursts out and says:[1] "Happy is the man who finds wisdom and is rich in discernment; for the acquiring of it is better than dealing in silver and gold, and first and purest are its fruits. My son, keep the law and hold to good counsel and it will be life to your soul and pleasant to your throat. Then you shall walk safely in your way and your foot will not stumble. If you sleep you will not be afraid. You will rest and your sleep will be sweet. Do not tremble at the sudden terror and the powers of the wicked rushing against you. For the Lord will be at your side and keep safe your foot so that you are not caught."

All this may be understood as follows: he is a blessed man who can find this unifying wisdom and can enrich his spiritual work with this loving intelligence and prudence of spirit, offering up his own blind feeling of his own being, all speculative knowledge from scholarship or nature put far from him. The buying of this spiritual wisdom and simple work is better than the getting of gold or silver. By gold and silver are understood, in the moral sense, all other bodily and spiritual knowledge which we get by spiritual searching and working with our natural senses beneath us, within us, or on the level with us, as we consider any of the qualities that belong to the being of God or of any created thing. He gives the reasons why it is better and says: "Its fruits are the first and purest". And no wonder since the fruit of this work is high spiritual wisdom, suddenly and freely raised up by the spirit inwardly in itself, undefined and very far from

[1] Proverbs III. 13, 14, 21–26.

fantasy, it cannot be controlled or be subject to the working of the natural intelligence. The natural intelligence, however wise and holy, may be called in comparison with this but feigned folly formed in fantasy, as far from the real truth when the spiritual sun shines, as the murkiness of the moonshine in a mist on a midwinter night is from the brightness of the sunshine in the clearest time of a midsummer day. "My son", he says, "take good care of this law and this counsel in which all the commandments and counsels, both of the Old Testament and the New, are truly and perfectly fulfilled without any special consideration of any one singularly by itself. For no other reason is this manner of working called a law but because it contains in itself completely all the branches and fruits of the law. For no other reason is this manner of working called a law but because it contains in itself completely all the branches and fruits of the law. For if it is looked at wisely, the foundation and strength of this work will be seen to be nothing else but the glorious gift of love in which, the Apostle teaches, all law is fulfilled. "The fullness of the law is Love". [1]

This loving law and life-giving counsel, if you keep it, will be as Solomon says, "life to your soul" within, in tenderness of love to your God and "grace to your countenance" without, in truest teaching and most becoming bodily behaviour to your fellow Christians in your outward form of living. On these two commandments, the one within the other without, [2] "hang all the law and the prophets", as Christ teaches—that is to say on the love of God and your neighbour. And therefore, when you are made thus perfect in your work both within and without, then you will go confidently, with grace your foundation and guide in the spiritual way, lovingly lifting up your bare blind being to the blessed being of your God,—two beings that are but one

[1] Romans XIII. 10.
[2] Matt. XXII. 40.

124

in grace though different in nature. "And the foot of your love shall not stumble". That is to say that once you have experience of your spiritual work in constancy of spirit, you will not so easily be hindered or drawn back by speculative questions posed by your curious senses as you are now at the beginning. Or else it means this: then shall the foot of your love neither stumble nor trip on any kind of fantasy caused by speculative searching of your senses. For in this work, as was said before, speculative searching of your natural senses is put far away from you and entirely forgotten for fear of fantasy or any feigned falsehood that may befall in this life: which in this work might befoul the bare feeling of your blind being and draw you away from the value of the work.

If any kind of special thought of anything excepting only your bare unquestioning being (which is your God and your aspiration) comes to your mind, then you are astray and drawn back to work in the deviousness and speculation of your senses, dispersing and separating you and your mind both from yourself and from your God. Therefore hold yourself whole and undispersed as far as you can by grace and the device of a spiritual constancy. For in this blind consideration of your bare being thus united with God, as I am telling you, you are to do all that you do: eat and drink, sleep and wake, move and sit, speak and be silent, lie down and get up, stand and kneel, run and ride, work and rest. This you must offer up every day to God as the most precious offering that you can make. It must be the principle of all your doings, whether they are active or contemplative. For, as Solomon says in the passage: "If you are asleep", in this blind consideration, to the noise and turmoil of the foul fiend, false world and frail flesh, "you shall not fear any peril"—nor any deception of the devil, because in this work he is utterly bewildered, blinded by his painful lack of knowledge and wildly wondering what you are doing. This does not matter, for you "shall graciously rest" in this loving unity of God and your soul "and your sleep shall be very sweet". For it will be spiritual food and inward strength both to your body and to your soul, as this same Solomon says soon afterwards:[1] "It is health to all weakness and sickness of the flesh",—and rightly, since all sickness and corruption fell upon the flesh when the soul lapsed from this work, and so shall all health come to the flesh when the soul, by the grace of Jesus who is the chief worker, rises to this same work again. This you can only hope to have by the mercy of Jesus and your own loving consent. Therefore I pray you, with Solomon here in this passage that you make a firm stand in this work, always bearing up to Him your loving consent in the eagerness of love. "And do not dread the sudden terror and powers of the wicked rushing upon you". That is, do not be dismayed by any anxious dread, though the devil come (as he will) with sudden fierceness, smiting and beating upon the walls of your house where you are sitting, or though he stir up any of his mighty assistants to rise and rush upon you suddenly without any warning. Be quite sure that it will be so, that whoever sets himself to work truly in this work shall indeed see or feel, taste smell or hear something frightening created by the devil in one of his outer senses; and all this is done to draw you down from the height of this precious work. Therefore take good care of your heart in the time of this torment, and incline with a trustful eagerness to the love of Our Lord.

"For the Lord will be at your side and guard your foot, that you be not caught." That is, the Lord will be at your side ready and near to help you and guard your foot (that is the ascent of your love, by which you go to God), so that you shall not be caught by any trick or guile of your enemies, the devil and his supporters, the world and the flesh. See, friend, so shall Our Lord and our Love in His might, wisdom and goodness aid, keep and defend all those

---

[1] Proverbs IV. 22.

who on account of the loving faith that they feel in Him will entirely leave off caring for themselves.

THE SIXTH CHAPTER

But where shall such a soul be found—so freely fastened and founded in the faith, so entirely humble in annihilating itself, so lovingly led and fed in the love of Our Lord; with full knowledge and feeling of His omnipotence, His unfathomable wisdom and His glorious goodness, and of how He is one in all and all in Him, so that without yielding up to God all that is of Him, by Him and in Him, a loving soul is never truly humbled in complete annihilation of itself? It is for this noble annihilation of itself in true humility and for exalting God as its all in perfect love, that it deserves to have God, (in whose love it is deeply immersed in the full and final forsaking of itself as nothing,—or less than nothing, if there can be less), mightily, wisely and well aiding, keeping and defending it from all adversities, bodily and spiritual, without any effort, care, toil or deliberation on its part.

Let go of your man-made objections, you half-humbled souls, and do not say, in your reasonable logic, that such a humble utter-forsaking of a man's care for himself when he feels himself thus touched by grace is any tempting of God, just because you feel in your mind that you dare not do so yourself. No, be content with your part, for it is sufficient for the saving of your souls in the active life, and leave alone other contemplative souls that dare act like this. Do not muse on or marvel at their words or their deeds although you think they pass beyond the course and common judgment of your reason.

Oh, for shame! How often do you read or hear a thing and give neither trust nor credence to it? I mean the thing that all the Fathers of the Church of old have written and taught before our time, and the thing that is the fruit and flower of

127

all Holy Scripture. It would seem either that you are blind
and are not able to receive with belief what you read or hear,
or else that you are touched with some secret kind of envy so
that you cannot believe that so great a good should fall to
your brethren when you are without it yourselves. You
were well advised to take care; for your enemy is devious
and intends to make you have more trust in your own
intelligence than in the old teaching of the true Fathers or the
working of the grace and will of Our Lord. How often have
you read and heard, and from how many men both holy and
wise and trustworthy, that as soon as Benjamin was born his
mother Rachel died? By Benjamin we understand contemplation, by Rachel reason. As soon as the soul is touched
by real contemplation, as it is in this noble annihilation of
itself and lofty acceptance of God as all, then truly all man's
reason dies. Since you have read this so often, not only in
one or two but in very many, very holy and trustworthy
writers, why do you not believe it? Or if you do believe it,
how dare you pillage and search with your reason Benjamin's words and deeds? By Benjamin is to be understood
all those who in excess of love are ravished above their
minds,—as the prophet says:[1] "There is little Benjamin, in
an ecstasy". Look to it then, that you be not like those
wretched women that slay their own children when they are
new-born. It is good to take care: do not couch your presumptuous spear as stoutly as you can against the might and
wisdom and will of Our Lord, nor through blindness and
lack of experience act as if you would bear Him down when
you most think you are holding Him up.

In the first beginnings of Holy Church, in time of persecution, many and various souls were so marvellously touched
by the sudden impact of grace that all at once, unprepared by
any other works, craftsmen threw down their tools and
children their textbooks in school, and ran out spon-

[1] Psalm 67 (68): verse 28 vulgate.

128

taneously to martyrdom with the saints. Why then should men not believe now, in time of peace, that God may, can, will and indeed does touch various souls suddenly by the grace of contemplation? This I believe He will do very graciously in chosen souls, for His goodness will be known in the end to the wonder of the world. Such a soul, annihilating itself for love and exalting God to be his all, shall through God's grace be kept from all overthrow by his spiritual and bodily enemies, without any trouble and toil on his part, by the goodness of God alone.

It is divinely reasonable that He should truly take care of all those who, concentrating on His love, forsake and care not to look after themselves. And no wonder that they are so marvellously taken care of, since they are so completely humbled in the boldness and strength of love.

Whoever dare not act like this and speaks against it, either the devil is in his breast, robbing him of the loving trust he should have in his God and the goodwill he should have to his fellow Christians, or else he is not as yet as perfectly humble as he needs to be,—I mean if he aims at the life which is truly contemplative. Therefore do not be abashed to be made thus humble for the Lord, nor so to sleep in this blind consideration of God as He is, away from all the noise of this wicked world, the false fiend and the frail flesh; for Our Lord will be ready to help you and guard your foot so that you shall not be taken.

The work is justly likened to sleep. For in sleep the use of the bodily senses has ceased, so that the body may take its full rest, feeding and strengthening the bodily nature. Even so in this spiritual sleep, the wanton questions of the untamed spiritual senses and imaginative reasoning are bound fast and utterly voided, so that the blessed soul may sleep quietly and rest in the loving contemplation of God as He is, feeding to the fill and strengthening the spiritual nature.

Therefore keep your senses under control as you offer up

this bare blind feeling of your own being, and always look (as I often say) that it be bare and not clad in any quality of your being. For if you clothe it with any quality, such as the worthiness of your being, or with any other particular condition that is your lot as a man, as compared with the being of any other creature; then immediately you give food to your senses, by which they gain occasion and strength to draw you to many things and to lose concentration, you never know how. Beware of this snare, I pray you.

THE SEVENTH CHAPTER

But now perhaps, in the curious speculation of your subtle mind, because it has no knowledge of this work, you may marvel at the manner of the work and hold it suspect; and that is not surprising, for you have up till now been too clever in your mind to acquire knowledge of any such action. Perhaps you ask in your heart how you should know whether this work is pleasing to God or not, and if it is pleasing, how it can be as pleasing as I say it is. In answer to this I say that this question springs from a subtle mind that will not in any way allow you to consent to this work until some concession is made to its curiosity by some good explanation.

Therefore I shall not refuse but I shall in part make myself like you, gratifying your proud mind, so that afterwards you may be like me, following my counsels without setting any limits to your humility: for as St. Bernard witnesses:[1] "Perfect humility sets no limits". You set limits to your humility when you will not implement the advice of your spiritual master unless your mind considers it the thing to do. Look: here you may see from my words that I desire to be your spiritual master,—and so I do and so I intend to be. I believe that it is love that urges me to this rather than any

---

[1] *Liber de Praecepto et Dispensatione* chap VI

ability that I feel in myself,—any depth of knowledge or skill in working or perfection of living. May God amend anything that is amiss, for He knows the whole, I only part.

And now, in order to give satisfaction to your proud mind in commanding this work, I will tell you truly that if a soul that is thus occupied had the tongue and language to say what it feels, then all the scholars in Christendom would wonder at its wisdom. Yes, and in comparison with it all their great scholarship would seem plain folly. So it is not surprising that I with my crude uncultivated tongue cannot tell you the value of this work: indeed, God forbid that it should be so debased and distorted by the wagging of a tongue of flesh. No! This may not be and surely will not be, and God forbid that I should want it so. For all that is spoken of it is not itself but of it. Now therefore, since we are unable to speak it, let us speak of it to the confusion of proud minds, and especially of yours, which is at least the sole occasion and the cause of my writing this letter.

First I ask you what is the perfection of man's soul, and what are the properties that pertain to this perfection? I answer on your behalf and say that the perfection of man's soul is nothing else but a union between God and itself in perfect love. This perfection is so high and pure in itself, beyond the comprehension of man, that it may not be known or perceived in itself; but where the properties that pertain to this perfection are truly seen and perceived, there it is likely that the substance will abound. Therefore if we are to declare the nobility of this spiritual exercise before all others, we must now know what are the properties that pertain to perfection.

The properties that pertain to perfection and which each perfect soul is bound to have are virtues: and if you will truly contemplate this work in your soul, and the property and condition of each individual virtue, you will find that all virtues are perfectly comprehended in it, without any distortion or corruption of your intent.

I shall not deal with any virtue in particular here, for it is not necessary. For they have been dealt with at large in various other places in my own writings.[1] For the same work, if it is properly understood, is that reverent affection and the fruit separated from the tree that I spoke about in my little "Epistle on Prayer". This is the Cloud of Unknowing; this is the secret love rooted in purity of spirit; this is the Ark of the Covenant. This is Denys' divinity, his wisdom and his treasure, his luminous darkness and his unknowing knowledge. This it is that reduces you to silence from thoughts as well as from words. This makes your prayers very short. In this you learn to forsake the world and despise it.

What is more, in this you are taught to forsake and despise yourself according to the teaching of Christ in the Gospel where He says:[2] "Whoever would come after Me, let him forsake himself, take up his cross and follow Me", as if He meant you to understand in accordance with our subject, "Whoever will come humbly not with Me but after Me to the bliss of Heaven or to the mount of perfection". For Christ went before by nature and we come after Him by grace. His nature is of more worth than grace and grace is of more worth than our nature. By this He lets us understand fully that we are in no way able to follow Him to the mount of perfection,—as ought to happen in this work,—unless we are inspired and led by grace; and this is the whole truth.

For you and all like you who read or hear this writing must fully understand that although I bid you thus plainly and boldly to set yourselves to this work, yet I feel without error or doubt that Almighty God with His grace must always be the principal instigator and worker, through intermediaries or without; and that you, and any like you, are only the consenters or recipients. I would only add that this consent and reception must, at the time of this work, be

---

[1] What follows are references to the author's other works.
[2] Matt. XVI. 24.

actively inclined and made ready for the work in purity of spirit, and fittingly borne up to your Sovereign, as you may learn by experience in the inward sight of your spirit.

Since it happens that God in His goodness stirs up and touches different souls differently,—some I mean through intermediaries, some without,—who then dares say that God does not stir you up, or any other like you who hears or reads this writing, through me alone as an intermediary, unworthy as I am, (saving His holy will in which He pleases to do as He pleases.)

So I believe it will be: the work itself will give proof when it is put to the test. Therefore I pray you make yourself ready to receive this grace from your Lord and hear what He says: "Whoever will come after Me" (in the manner aforesaid) "let him forsake himself". I ask you, how can a man more forsake himself and the world, and more despise himself and the world, than by disdaining to think of any quality of their being?

THE EIGHTH CHAPTER

For you must thoroughly understand that though I bid you to forget all things but the blind feeling of your own being, yet nevertheless my purpose is, and has been from the beginning, that you should forget the feeling of your own being in the feeling of the being of God; and for this reason I proved to you in the beginning that God is your being. But I thought you were not yet fit to be suddenly lifted up to the spiritual feeling of the being of God, immature as you are in your spiritual feelings, and therefore I let you climb there by degrees.

I bade you first to gnaw upon the bare blind feeling of your own being until such time as you became fit to receive the lofty feeling of God by spiritual perseverance in this secret work. For your intention and desire must always be to

THE LETTER OF PRIVATE DIRECTION

feel God in this work. For although I bid you at the beginning, on account of your inexperience and spiritual immaturity, to wrap and clothe the feeling of your God in the feeling for yourself; yet afterwards, when by perseverance you had been made more wise in purity of spirit, you shall strip, spoil, and completely unclothe yourself of all kinds of feelings of yourself, that you may be able to be clothed with the gracious feeling of God Himself. This is the true condition of the perfect lover, that he wholly and completely strips himself of himself for the sake of that which he loves, and does not allow or permit himself to be clothed except in that which he loves,—and that not only for a time, but endlessly to be enfolded therein to the full and final forgetting of himself. This is the work of love that none may know but he who feels it. This is the lesson of Our Lord when He says: "Whoever will love Me let him forsake himself"; as if He said: "Let him strip himself of himself, if he would truly be clothed in Me who am the ample garment of love and eternity that never shall have an end."

Therefore whenever you consider your work and see and feel that it is yourself that you feel and not God, you must be filled with sincere sorrow and heartily long for the feeling of God; always desiring without ceasing to forget the woeful knowledge and foul feeling of your own blind being, and be eager to flee from yourself as from poison. Then do you forsake and thoroughly despise yourself as your Lord bids you. And then when you desire so single-mindedly, not to cease to be, for that would be madness and an insult to God, but to forego the knowledge and feeling of your being, as must always happen if God's love is to be felt perfectly as far as it can be in this life: and when you see and feel that in no way can you come to your purpose, for however busy you may be there will always follow and go with your doings a bare feeling of your blind being, (except only for a very occasional short period when God will let you feel Himself in abundance of love); and this bare feeling of your blind

134

being will always push in above, between you and your God, as in the beginning the qualities of your own being will push between you and yourself; then you will think that the burden of yourself is very heavy and exceedingly painful. Yes! May Jesus help you then, for then you have need. All the misery that lies outside is as nothing compared with that. For you are then yourself a cross to yourself, and this is the true work and way to Our Lord as He Himself says: "Let him bear his cross" first in the suffering of himself, and afterwards "follow me" to bliss and the mount of perfection, tasting the tenderness of My love and the divine feeling of Myself.

Here you may see that you must sorrowfully desire to forego the feeling of yourself and painfully bear the burden of yourself as a cross before you can be united with God in spiritual feeling of Himself, Who is perfect love. And here to some extent and in part, according as you are touched and spiritually marked with this grace, you may see and feel the value of this work beyond all others.

THE NINTH CHAPTER

Now I pray you tell me how you could come to this work by the use of your intelligence? Never,—nor yet by your fair and learned, your clever and elaborate fancies and meditations, even though they be about your wretched mode of life, the Passion of Christ, the joys of Our Lady or of all the saints and angels in Heaven, or indeed about any quality, refinement of condition that appertains to your own being or that of God.

Certainly I would rather have such a bare blind feeling of myself as I touched on before: not of my actions but of myself. (Many men call their actions themselves, but it is not so. For I that do the actions am one thing, my actions that are performed another. It is the same with God: He Himself is

135

one thing, His works are another). I would rather that my heart should break with weeping for my lack of feeling of God and for the painful burden of myself, and kindle my desire with love and longing for the awareness of God, than all the elaborate fancies and meditations that a man can tell, or find written in a book, however holy they may be or however fair they may appear to the subtle eye of the speculative mind.

Nonetheless, these fair meditations are the truest way that a sinner may take at the start to the spiritual feeling of himself and of God. I would think it impossible, as far as man's understanding goes,—(although God may do what He wishes)—for a sinner to come to rest in the spiritual awareness of himself and God, unless he first saw and felt in imagination and meditation the bodily actions of himself and God, and therein sorrowed at what was sorrowful and rejoiced in what was joyful. Whoever does not come in by this way does not really come in: therefore he must stand outside, and does so, when he thinks he is most truly inside. For many think that they are inside the spiritual door and yet they are standing outside; and they will do so until the time when they humbly seek the door. Some there are that seek the door soon and come in sooner than some others; this depends upon the doorkeeper, clearly without worth or merit on their part. The house of the spirit is marvellous. For the Lord is Himself not only the doorkeeper but also the door; the doorkeeper in His Godhead, the door in His Manhood, as He Himself says in the Gospel:[1] "I am the door. If anyone enters by Me, he shall be saved; he shall go out and go in and he shall find pasture. But he who does not come in through the door but climbs in elsewhere is a thief and a robber." You may understand this in accordance with our subject: "I am Almighty by My Godhead, and may rightly as doorkeeper let in whom I will and by what way I will; but

[1] John X.

136

wish there to be a general clear way and open entrance for all who will come, so that none may have the excuse of not knowing the way: and therefore I have clothed Myself in the common nature of man and made Myself so available that I am the door in My Manhood, and whoever enters through Me shall be saved.''

Those enter by the door who contemplate the Passion of Christ and sorrow for their wickedness which is the cause of that Passion, bitterly reproaching themselves who have deserved punishment and not suffered it, and feeling pity and compassion for the good Lord who suffered so vilely and never deserved to: and who therefore lift up their hearts to the love and goodness of His Godhead in which He condescended to make Himself so low in our mortal manhood. All these enter by the door and they will be saved, whether they go in, contemplating the love and goodness of the Godhead, or go out, contemplating the agony of His manhood. They shall find spiritual food of devotion sufficient, plentiful and abounding for the help and saving of their souls although they do not penetrate further in this life.

Whoever does not enter by the door but climbs otherwise to perfection by subtle searching and speculative fantastic working in his wild and unruly senses, leaving the aforesaid general clear entrance and the true counsel of spiritual fathers; whoever he may be, he is not only a thief in the night but a prowler by day. A thief in the night because he goes in the darkness of sin, and is more inclined in his presumption to the independent judgement of his own mind and will than to any true counsel or this general clear way. He is a prowler by day because, under the appearance of pure spiritual living, he secretly picks up the outward signs and words of contemplation but he does not get the fruit. So when he feels in himself sometimes a pleasant longing, slight though it is, to come near to God, he is blinded by its appearance, and thinks that everything he does is good enough, when it is the most perilous course there can be,—that a young man follow the violence of his desire unguided by counsel especially when he is set on the one purpose of scaling the heights, not only above himself but above the ordinary way of Christian men which I call, as Christ teaches, the door to devotion and the truest entrance to contemplation that there can be in this life.

THE TENTH CHAPTER

But now to proceed with the subject of this letter as it especially applies to you alone and to all others that are like you in disposition. Supposing this is the door, shall a man when he has found the door stand at it or just inside it, and come no further in? I answer on your behalf, and say that it is good that he should continue to do so until the great rust of his rough bodily nature is to a great extent rubbed away, as his director and his conscience bear witness; and always especially until he is called further in by the secret teaching of the Spirit of God.

This teaching is the readiest and most certain witness that may be had in this life of the calling and drawing of a soul further in to the more special workings of grace. The evidence of this grace touching a man may be this: if he feels, in the course of his continual religious exercise, as it were a growing desire to come near God in this life,—it may be by a special spiritual feeling which he has heard men tell of, or else found written in books. But he who does not feel himself stirred when reading or hearing of spiritual work, and especially during each day's spiritual exercise, by a growing desire to come near God, let him still stand at the door as a man called to salvation but not yet to perfection. I warn you of one thing, whoever you may be who read or hear this letter, and especially in this place where I make a distinction between those who are called to salvation and those who are called to perfection: to whichever state you feel your calling to be, see that you neither judge nor discuss the deeds of God or of man—except for what concerns yourself alone—not, for instance, whom He stirs up and calls to perfection and whom He does not call; or the short-ness of the time, or why He calls one rather than another. If you would not go astray, look to it that you do not judge, but only hear and understand. If you are called, give praise to God and pray that you may not fall; and if you are not yet called, pray humbly that He may call you when it is His will. But do not try to teach Him what He should do. Let Him alone: He is mighty and wise and ready enough to do what is best for you and for all who love Him. Be content with your lot whichever you have. You have no grounds for com-plaint, both are precious. The first is good and is essential: the second is better, let him get it who may. Or to speak more truly, whoever is got by grace and called thereto by Our Lord. For we in our pride may press forward and stumble at the end. Certainly without Him there is nothing we can do, as He Himself says:[1] "Without Me you can do nothing." Which you may understand as: "Without Me first stirring you up and acting as prime mover, while you only consent and allow it, you are not able to do anything that is perfectly pleasing to Me"—as in a manner the work about which I am writing should be.

I say all this to confute the presumptuous error of those who in the subtlety of their scholarship and natural intel-ligence wish always to be principal workers themselves, God only allowing it and consenting to it; whereas the exact opposite is the truth in contemplative matters. For in these alone, all the speculative knowledge acquired by scholarship and natural ingenuity must be completely laid aside so that God may be the chief worker. However in lawful matters of the active life, men's scholarship and natural ingenuity are to work side by side with God, once granted His consent in

[1] John XV. 5.

spirit as declared by these three witnesses: Scripture, direction, and ordinary behaviour in accordance with nature, state, age and disposition. Nor shall a man follow the impulse of the spirit, however pleasant and however holy it may seem to be (I mean in the affairs of active life), unless it is within the range of his scholarship and natural knowledge: not even though it be very strongly supported by all or any of the three witnesses aforesaid. And indeed, it is very reasonable that a man be more than his works: for which reason by the law and ordinance of Holy Church no man shall be admitted to prelacy, which is the highest degree of active living, unless it is shown by the testimony of a thorough examination that the duties of his office are within the range of his abilities.

So in the affairs of the active life, a man's learning and natural ability will play the leading part in the work, with God's gracious consent and the approval of these three witnesses. And rightly so, for all the affairs of active life are within the scope of and in the charge of men's wisdom. But in contemplative matters, the loftiest wisdom that a man, as man, can have must be completely subjected so that God may be the mainspring of the work and man only consents and receives it.

And so I understand the words of the Gospel: "Without Me you can do nothing", in one way for those in the active life, in another for contemplatives. For those in the active life there must be God's permission or consent, or both, if anything is to be done, whether it is lawful and pleasing to Him or not. In contemplatives, God as chief worker asks of them nothing but sufferance and consent. So to sum up: in all our actions, lawful or unlawful, active or contemplative, we can do nothing without Him. He is with us in sin only by sufferance, not by consent, to our final damnation if we do not humbly mend our ways. In actions that are both active and lawful He is with us both by sufferance and consent: to our shame if we backslide, and to our great merit if we carry

140

it through. In contemplative works He is with us as chief instigator and worker, ourselves only accepting and consenting, to our great perfection and the spiritual uniting of our souls to Him in perfect love. And thus since all men alive can be divided into three categories, sinners, actives and contemplatives, this saying may be applied to all the world in general: "Without Me", only permitting but not consenting, as in sinners, or else both permitting and consenting, as in actives, or—best of all—as principal instigator and worker, as in contemplatives, "you can do nothing".

Here are many words and little substance. But I have told you all this to let you know in what things you must set your intelligence to work and in what you must not; and how God is with you in one kind of action and how in another. And after all, knowing this you may avoid mistakes into which you might have fallen if it had not been explained. So since it has been said, let it stand, although it has little to do with our subject,—to which I now return.

THE ELEVENTH CHAPTER

You may ask this question: "Tell me, if you would be so kind, by what sign, or signs if you prefer, I may most quickly know, without any mistake, whether this growing desire that I feel in my work each day and this pleasant impulse that I have on reading or hearing of this subject be truly a call from God to the more special work of grace which is the subject of this letter; or whether it is a nourishing and feeding of my spirit to stay still and work on in my ordinary grace that you call the door and the general entrance for all Christian men?"

This I will answer as best I can, though feebly. You can clearly perceive that I give you here in this letter two kinds of evidence by which you are to test your spiritual calling by God to this work, one within, the othr without. Neither of

141

these two, as I think, will be absolutely sufficient in this case without the other. But where they are both together united and in agreement then your evidence is quite sufficient without any chance of failure.

The first of these two pieces of evidence, the one that is within, is the growing desire that you feel in each day's work. About this desire you must know this much, that although the desire is the work of the soul which is blind in itself,—the desire is to the soul as handling and walking are to the body, and handling and walking are blind works of the body as you know well,—although the work of the desire be blind, yet there comes with it and follows it a kind of spiritual insight, which is in part the cause and the means of furthering your desire. Examine then carefully your daily exercise, what it is in itself; if it is the remembrance of your own wretchedness, the Passion of Christ, or any other such thing as belongs to the general entrance of Christian men as mentioned before, and if the spiritual insight that comes with and follows after your blind desire arises from these ordinary considerations, then certainly this is a sign to me that the growth of the desire is but a nourishing and feeding of your spirit to remain still, and to work on in common grace, not a call or impulse from God to any more special grace.

The second evidence, the one that is without, is a pleasant impulse that you feel on hearing or reading of the subject. I call this evidence from without because it comes from without, through the windows of your bodily senses, by hearing and seeing while you are reading. If it does not last or continue with you beyond the time of the reading or hearing of it, but ceases then or else soon after, so that it is not present with you when you go to sleep or wake up; and especially if it does not follow you into your daily exercise as it were coming and squeezing between you and your prayer, stirring up and leading on your desire; then in my opinion it is truly a sign that this pleasant impulse that you feel on hearing or reading of this subject is but the natural pleasure that every Christian soul has on hearing or reading the truth,— especially that which touches deftly and declares truly the properties that belong to the soul of man, and especially to God. And it is not a spiritual imparting of grace, nor a call from God to any more special work of grace other than that which is the door and entry for ordinary Christian men.

But if it happens that the pleasant impulse that you feel on hearing or reading of this subject is so all-encompassing in itself that it goes with you to bed and rises with you in the morning and follows you all through the day and in all that you do; if it cuts you off from your usual daily exercise, inserting itself between this and you, and so accompanies and follows your desire that you think that it is all one desire, and you cannot think what it is that changes your bearing and makes your demeanour decorous; if while it lasts every-thing pleases you and nothing can grieve you; if you would run a thousand miles to converse by word of mouth with one who you knew had really felt this, and yet when you come there you can find nothing to say, let others say what they will, for you have no desire to speak of anything but this; if your words be few but full of substance and fire; if a short word from your mouth contains a world of wisdom yet seems but foolishness to those that depend on their human reason; if your silence is comforting, your words very helpful, your prayer is secret, your self-esteem free from conceit, your behaviour humble, your humour entirely without malice, what you wish for is the pleasure of playing with a child. If you like to be alone and sit by yourself, for you think that men would hinder you unless they were working with you; if you do not wish to read a book or hear it read unless it is about this work: then your inward evidence and your outer are both in agreement and united in one.

THE TWELFTH CHAPTER

Furthermore, if both these evidences and all the above conditions cease for a time after you have had any or all of them, and you think that you are left bare as it were, both of the feeling of his new enthusiasm and of your old accustomed work, and that you have fallen between the two, not having either but being without both; do not be too dejected over this, but endure it humbly and await patiently the will of Our Lord. For now you are on the spiritual sea (as I should describe it), voyaging from the bodily to the spiritual.

Many great storms and temptations may arise at this time, and you do not know where to run for help. All feeling of ordinary grace and special grace have left you. Do not be too afraid, though you think you have grounds for fear. Have loving trust in Our Lord,—though what you can muster at the time may be but little,—for He is not far away. He may give you His attention very soon and touch you again with more fervent impulse of that same grace than you ever felt at any time before. Then you are made whole, and everything seems to you as good as can be while it lasts. Then suddenly before you know it everything is gone and you are left stripped bare in the boat, blown blundering hither and thither, you do not know where or whither. Do not be dismayed, for He will come again when He pleases, very soon, I promise you, to relieve you and doughtily deliver you from all your despondence more excellently than He ever did before. Yes: and if He goes again afterwards He will return again; and each time, if you bear yourself humbly in your sufferings, He will come more excellently and bring you more joy than the time before. He does all this because He would have you made as pliant to His will spiritually as a kid glove is to your hand bodily.

Sometimes He goes and sometimes He comes and in this twofold work He will doubly test you in secret and mould

144

you to His own work. By the withdrawing of your fervour, which you think is His going away although it is not so, He will thoroughly test your patience. For you must understand very well that although God sometimes withdraws these sensible pleasures, these fervent feelings and burning desires, yet He never withdraws His grace from His chosen. For truly I do not believe that His spiritual grace can ever be withdrawn from His chosen ones who have once been touched by it, unless mortal sin were the cause. But all these sensible pleasures, fervent feelings and burning desires, which in themselves are not grace but signs of grace, are often withdrawn to test our patience and often for our many other spiritual profits, more than we can know. For grace in itself is so lofty, pure and spiritual that it cannot be felt in our sensible part; the signs of it may be, but not grace itself. So the Lord will sometimes withdraw your sensible fervour both for the increasing and testing of your patience; and not for this purpose alone but for many others which I will not deal with here: I continue with our subject. By the excellence, frequency and increase of these sensible feelings aforesaid (which you think are His coming, although it be not so), He nourishes and feeds your spirit to persevere and live in love and worship of Him: thus by patience in the absence of these sensible feelings, the signs of grace, and by that life-giving nourishment and that loving feeding of your spirit in their presence, He will make you in both together joyously lissom and pleasantly pliant to that perfection and spiritual unity with His will which is perfect love: so much so that you will be as glad and as happy to forego such sensible feelings if it be God's will for you to have them and feel them continually all your lifetime. At this time your love is both chaste and perfect: at this time you both see your God and your love and nakedly feel Him by spiritual union with His love in the point of your spirit. You feel Him as He is in Himself, but blindlly as it must be in this life, utterly stripped of yourself, your nakedness clothed in Him as He is—unclothed and not wrapped round with any of those sensual feelings, however sweet and holy they be, that may occur in this life. In purity of spirit He is properly and perfectly perceived and felt in Himself as He is, far removed from any fantasy or false opinion that may occur in this life.

This sight and feeling of God in Himself as He is can no more be separated from God in Himself (to your understanding who feel and see) than God Himself can be separated from His own being, and they are but one both in substance and in nature. So as God cannot be separated from His being owing to this unity in nature, so the soul that thus sees and feels cannot be separated from that which it sees and feels owing to unity in grace.

Thus then and by these signs you may to some extent know and in part test the manner and excellence of your calling and the stirring of grace in your spiritual work within, and in the reading and hearing of the matter without. And then, from the time that you or any other person like you in spirit have truly had experience of all these signs or any of them,—(for in the first instance only very few are so specially touched and marked with this grace that at once or suddenly in their true feelings they have proof of them all; but it is sufficient to have one or two of them, though a man may not have all of them at first), if therefore you feel that you have true experience of one or two approved as true by examination of Scripture, your spiritual director and your conscience, then it is helpful for you sometimes to cease from these elaborate meditations and clever imaginations of the qualities of your being and God's and of your works and God's (by which your mind has been fed and through which you have been led from worldliness and bodiliness to your present capacity for grace), and to learn how you are to be occupied spiritually in the feeling of yourself and of God, about whom you have learned so much already by thinking of and imagining your doings.

THE THIRTEENTH CHAPTER

Christ gave an example of this in His life; for if in truth there had been no greater perfection in this life than considering and loving His manhood, I believe He would not have ascended into Heaven while this world lasted, nor withdrawn His bodily presence from His special lovers on earth.

But there was a higher perfection that a man could have in this life, that is to say a pure spiritual feeling in love of His Godhead. Therefore when his disciples grudged foregoing His bodily presence (as you do to some extent, and in a way, grudge giving up your speculative meditation and abstruse clever reasoning), He said to them that[1] it was helpful for them that He went away from them bodily. On these words the holy doctor comments:[2] "Unless His human form was withdrawn from our bodily eyes, our spiritual eyes could not be fastened on the love of His Godhead." So, I tell you that it is sometimes helpful to leave off the speculative work of your mind and learn to taste something of the love of God in your spiritual feeling.

You are to come to this feeling by the way that I describe to you with the help of grace going before. This is the way: that you always and without ceasing incline towards the bare feeling of yourself, continually offering your being to God as the most precious offering that you can make. But see, as I have often said, that it be bare, for fear of deception. If it be bare, then it will be very painful for you at the start to remain therein for any length of time,—for as I have said before, your senses will find that there is no food for them in it. But that does not matter; indeed, I prefer it so. Let them fast awhile I beg you from their natural delight in their learning. For while it is well said that man by nature desires

[1] John XVI. 7.
[2] St. Augustine, Sermon CXL III

to know,[1] yet certainly he cannot taste of spiritual feeling in God except by grace, however much knowledge he may have, natural or acquired.

Therefore I beg you to seek after feeling rather than knowledge. For knowledge often leads us astray through pride, but humble loving affection cannot beguile you.[2] "Knowledge puffs up, but love builds up". In knowledge is toil, in affection rest. At this you may say: "What rest is this that you are speaking about? For it seems to me that it is toil and pain and no rest at all: when I set myself to do as you say I find pain and strife on all sides. On one side my senses would bid me go away and I will not; on the other I wish to feel God and be without the feeling of myself and I cannot. So strife and pain are on all sides. This seems to me a queer sort of rest you are speaking about".

To which I reply that you are not used to the work and therefore it is more painful for you. But if you were accustomed to it, and knew by experience what profit is in it, you would not willingly leave it for all the bodily joy and rest in this world. And yet it is great toil and pain too. But I call it rest because the soul is not in doubt about what it should do: the soul is made sure, (I mean during the period of this work), that it will not go far astray.

[3]Therefore with humility and fervent desire continue in this work, which begins in this life and in everlasting life will never end. I pray almighty Jesus that He bring to this everlasting life all those whom He has redeemed with His precious blood.

Amen

Here ends the Letter of Private Direction.

---

[1] The opening of Aristotle's metaphysics

[2] 1 Cor. VIII. 1.

[3] This last paragraph is missing in some manuscripts but see Introduction.